THE
AMERICAN SATIRIST

THE WITTY WRITINGS
OF MARK TWAIN

By

MARK TWAIN

Read & Co.

Copyright © 2020 Read & Co. Books

This edition is published by Read & Co. Books,
an imprint of Read & Co.

This book is copyright and may not be reproduced or copied in any
way without the express permission of the publisher in writing.

British Library Cataloguing-in-Publication Data
A catalogue record for this book is available
from the British Library.

Read & Co. is part of Read Books Ltd.
For more information visit
www.readandcobooks.co.uk

CONTENTS

3

MARK TWAIN

Samuel Langhorne Clemens, better known by his pseudonym *Mark Twain,* was born on 30 November, 1835 in Florida, Missouri, USA. He was born the day after a visit by Halley's Comet, and died the day following its subsequent return in 1910.

He is best known for the novels *The Adventures of Tom Sawyer* (1876) and its sequel, *Adventures of Huckleberry Finn* (1885), the latter often referred to as 'the Great American Novel'.

Hailed as 'the father of American literature' by William Faulkner, Twain was a friend of presidents, performers, entrepreneurs and royalty. His wit and satire endeared him to peers and critics alike. Twain spent most of his childhood in Hannibal, Missouri, which provided the inspirational setting for much of his later works. It was here that Twain started writing, contributing articles to his older brother, Orion's newspaper. After a brief, unsuccessful, spell mining in Nevada and California, twain returned to writing – penning *The Celebrated Jumping Frog of Calaveras County* in 1865. This was a humorous tale based on a story heard at a mining camp in California, and won Twain international attention. Five years later, Twain married Olivia Langdon, the sister of Charles Langdon, a man whom Twain met on a trip to the Middle East.

Upon Langdon showing a picture of his sister Olivia to Twain, Twain claimed to have fallen in love with her at first sight. Through Olivia, Twain met many prominent liberals, socialists and political activists, including Harriet Beecher Stowe, the abolitionist and author, as well as the utopian socialist, William Dean Howells. These connections deeply influenced Twain's later political outlook, remaining firmly anti-imperialist, anti-organised religion, an abolitionist and a steady supporter of the labour movement. Twain and Olivia had three daughters,

Susy, Clara and Jean, and one son, Langdon. Unfortunately Langdon died whilst he was still in infancy. The family spent many happy summers at Quarry Farm - Olivia's sister's home on the outskirts of New York, where Twain wrote many of his classic novels; *The Adventures* and *Huckleberry Finn*, as well as *The Prince and the Pauper* (1881), *Life on the Mississippi* (1883) and *A Connecticut Yankee in King Arthur's Court* (1889). Despite these successes, financial as well as literary, Twain lost a great deal of money through investing in new technologies. His love of science and invention led him to invest a massive 300,000 dollars (about 8 million dollars today) in the *Paige typesetting machine*. This mechanical marvel was made redundant before it was even completed however, by the *Linotype* machine, and Twain lost his entire investment. As a result of this, on the advice from a friend, Twain filed for Bankruptcy. Fortunately, he was heavily in demand as a featured speaker, and embarked on a massive worldwide lecture tour in July 1895 to pay off all his creditors. After nearly five years travelling, Twain returned to America having earned enough money to pay off his debts. On his homecoming, Twain sadly suffered a period of deep depression, which began on his daughter Susy's death in 1896, and worsened on the death of his wife in 1904 and his other daughter Jean in 1909. Twain died of a heart attack on 21 April, 1910, in Redding, Connecticut. He had predicted his death, the day after Halley's comets closest approach to Earth; 'It will be the greatest disappointment of my life if I don't go out with Halley's Comet. The Almighty has said, no doubt: 'Now here are these two unaccountable freaks; they came in together, they must go out together."

He is buried at Woodlawn Cemetery, Elmira, New York.

THE AWFUL
GERMAN LANGUAGE

A little learning makes the whole world kin.

—*PROVERBS XXXII, 7.*

I went often to look at the collection of curiosities in Heidelberg Castle, and one day I surprised the keeper of it with my German. I spoke entirely in that language. He was greatly interested; and after I had talked a while he said my German was very rare, possibly a "unique"; and wanted to add it to his museum.

If he had known what it had cost me to acquire my art, he would also have known that it would break any collector to buy it. Harris and I had been hard at work on our German during several weeks at that time, and although we had made good progress, it had been accomplished under great difficulty and annoyance, for three of our teachers had died in the mean time. A person who has not studied German can form no idea of what a perplexing language it is.

Surely there is not another language that is so slipshod and systemless, and so slippery and elusive to the grasp. One is washed about in it, hither and thither, in the most helpless way; and when at last he thinks he has captured a rule which offers firm ground to take a rest on amid the general rage and turmoil of the ten parts of speech, he turns over the page and reads, "Let the pupil make careful note of the following *Exceptions.*" He runs his eye down and finds that there are more exceptions to the rule than instances of it. So overboard he goes again, to hunt for another Ararat and find another quicksand. Such has been, and continues to be, my experience. Every time I think I have got one of these four confusing "cases" where I am master of it, a seemingly insignificant preposition intrudes itself into my sentence, clothed with an awful and unsuspected power, and crumbles the ground from under me. For instance, my book inquires after a certain bird—(it is always inquiring after things which are of no sort of consequence to anybody): "Where is the bird?" Now the answer to this question—according to the book— is that the bird is waiting in the blacksmith shop on account of the rain. Of course no bird would do that, but then you must stick to the book. Very well, I begin to cipher out the German for that answer. I begin at the wrong end, necessarily, for that is the German idea. I say to myself, "*regen* (rain) is masculine—or maybe it is feminine—or possibly neuter—it is too much trouble to look now. Therefore, it is either *der* (the) Regen, or *die* (the) Regen, or *das* (the) Regen, according to which gender it may turn out to be when I look. In the interest of science, I will cipher it out on the hypothesis that it is masculine. Very well—then *the* rain is *der* Regen, if it is simply in the quiescent state of being *mentioned*, without enlargement or discussion—Nominative case; but if this rain is lying around, in a kind of a general way on the ground, it is then definitely located, it is *doing something*— that is, *resting* (which is one of the German grammar's ideas of doing something), and this throws the rain into the Dative case, and makes it *dem* Regen. However, this rain is not resting, but is doing something *actively*,—it is falling—to interfere with the bird, likely—and this indicates *movement*, which has the effect of sliding it into the Accusative case and changing *dem* Regen into *den* Regen." Having completed the grammatical horoscope of this matter, I answer up confidently and state in German that the bird is staying in the blacksmith shop "wegen (on account of) *den* Regen." Then the teacher lets me softly down with the remark that whenever the word "wegen" drops into a sentence, it *always* throws that subject into the *genitive* case, regardless of consequences—and therefore this bird stayed in the blacksmith shop "wegen *des* Regens."

N.B.—I was informed, later, by a higher authority, that there was an "exception" which permits one to say "wegen *den* Regen" in certain peculiar and complex circumstances, but that this exception is not extended to anything *but* rain.

There are ten parts of speech, and they are all troublesome. An average sentence, in a German newspaper, is a sublime and impressive curiosity; it occupies a quarter of a column; it contains all the ten parts of speech—not in regular order, but mixed; it is built mainly of compound words constructed by the writer on the spot, and not to be found in any dictionary—six or seven words compacted into one, without joint or seam— that is, without hyphens; it treats of fourteen or fifteen different subjects, each enclosed in a parenthesis of its own, with here and there extra parentheses, making pens within pens: finally, all the parentheses and reparentheses are massed together between a couple of king-parentheses, one of which is placed in the first line of the majestic sentence and the other in the middle of the last line of it—*after which comes the verb*, and you find out for the first time what the man has been talking about; and after the verb—merely by way of ornament, as far as I can make out—the writer shovels in "*haben sind gewesen gehabt haven geworden sein,*" or words to that effect, and the monument is finished. I suppose that this closing hurrah is in the nature of the flourish to a man's signature—not necessary, but pretty. German books are easy enough to read when you hold them before the looking-glass or stand on your head—so as to reverse the construction— but I think that to learn to read and understand a German newspaper is a thing which must always remain an impossibility to a foreigner.

Yet even the German books are not entirely free from attacks of the Parenthesis distemper—though they are usually so mild as to cover only a few lines, and therefore when you at last get down to the verb it carries some meaning to your mind because you are able to remember a good deal of what has gone before.

Now here is a sentence from a popular and excellent German novel—with a slight parenthesis in it. I will make a perfectly literal translation, and throw in the parenthesis-marks and some hyphens for the assistance of the reader—though in the original there are no parenthesis-marks or hyphens, and the reader is left to flounder through to the remote verb the best way he can:

"But when he, upon the street, the (in-satin-and-silk-covered-now-very-unconstrained-after-the-newest-fashioned-dressed) government counselor's wife *met*," etc., etc. [1]

That is from *The Old Mamselle's Secret*, by Mrs. Marlitt. And that sentence is constructed upon the most approved German model. You observe how far that verb is from the reader's base of operations; well, in a German newspaper they put their verb away over on the next page; and I have heard that sometimes after stringing along the exciting preliminaries and parentheses for a column or two, they get in a hurry and have to go to press without getting to the verb at all. Of course, then, the reader is left in a very exhausted and ignorant state.

We have the Parenthesis disease in our literature, too; and one may see cases of it every day in our books and newspapers: but with us it is the mark and sign of an unpracticed writer or a cloudy intellect, whereas with the Germans it is doubtless the mark and sign of a practiced pen and of the presence of that sort of luminous intellectual fog which stands for clearness among these people. For surely it is *not* clearness—it necessarily can't be clearness. Even a jury would have penetration enough to discover that. A writer's ideas must be a good deal confused, a good deal out of line and sequence, when he starts out to say that a man met a counselor's wife in the street, and then right in the midst of this so simple undertaking halts these approaching people and makes them stand still until he jots

---

1   Wenn er aber auf der Strasse der in Sammt und Seide gehuellten jetz sehr ungenirt nach der neusten mode gekleideten Regierungsrathin begegnet.

down an inventory of the woman's dress. That is manifestly absurd. It reminds a person of those dentists who secure your instant and breathless interest in a tooth by taking a grip on it with the forceps, and then stand there and drawl through a tedious anecdote before they give the dreaded jerk. Parentheses in literature and dentistry are in bad taste.

The Germans have another kind of parenthesis, which they make by splitting a verb in two and putting half of it at the beginning of an exciting chapter and the *other half* at the end of it. Can any one conceive of anything more confusing than that? These things are called "separable verbs." The German grammar is blistered all over with separable verbs; and the wider the two portions of one of them are spread apart, the better the author of the crime is pleased with his performance. A favorite one is *reiste ab*—which means departed. Here is an example which I culled from a novel and reduced to English:

"The trunks being now ready, he *de-* after kissing his mother and sisters, and once more pressing to his bosom his adored Gretchen, who, dressed in simple white muslin, with a single tuberose in the ample folds of her rich brown hair, had tottered feebly down the stairs, still pale from the terror and excitement of the past evening, but longing to lay her poor aching head yet once again upon the breast of him whom she loved more dearly than life itself, *parted*."

However, it is not well to dwell too much on the separable verbs. One is sure to lose his temper early; and if he sticks to the subject, and will not be warned, it will at last either soften his brain or petrify it. Personal pronouns and adjectives are a fruitful nuisance in this language, and should have been left out. For instance, the same sound, *sie*, means *you*, and it means *she*, and it means *her*, and it means *it*, and it means *they*, and it means *them*. Think of the ragged poverty of a language which has to make one word do the work of six—and a poor little weak thing of only three letters at that. But mainly, think of the exasperation of never knowing which of these meanings the speaker is trying to convey. This explains why, whenever a person says *sie* to me, I generally try to kill him, if a stranger.

Now observe the Adjective. Here was a case where simplicity would have been an advantage; therefore, for no other reason, the inventor of this language complicated it all he could. When we wish to speak of our "good friend or friends," in our enlightened tongue, we stick to the one form and have no trouble or hard feeling about it; but with the German tongue it is different. When a German gets his hands on an adjective, he declines it, and keeps on declining it until the common sense is all declined out of it. It is as bad as Latin. He says, for instance:

SINGULAR

Nominative—Mein gut*er* Freund, my good friend.
Genitives—Mein*es* Gut*en* Freund*es*, of my good friend.
Dative—Mein*em* gut*en* Freund, to my good friend.
Accusative—Mein*en* gut*en* Freund, my good friend.

PLURAL

N.—Mein*e* gut*en* Freund*e*, my good friends.
G.—Mein*er* gut*en* Freund*e*, of my good friends.
D.—Mein*en* gut*en* Freund*en*, to my good friends.
A.—Mein*e* gut*en* Freund*e*, my good friends.

Now let the candidate for the asylum try to memorize those variations, and see how soon he will be elected. One might better go without friends in Germany than take all this trouble about them. I have shown what a bother it is to decline a good (male) friend; well this is only a third of the work, for there is a variety of new distortions of the adjective to be learned when the object is feminine, and still another when the object is neuter. Now there are more adjectives in this language than there are black cats in Switzerland, and they must all be as elaborately declined as the examples above suggested. Difficult?—troublesome?—these words cannot describe it. I heard a Californian student in Heidelberg say, in one of his calmest moods, that he would rather decline two drinks than one German adjective.

The inventor of the language seems to have taken pleasure in complicating it in every way he could think of. For instance, if one is casually referring to a house, *haus*, or a horse, *pferd*, or a dog, *hund*, he spells these words as I have indicated; but if he is referring to them in the Dative case, he sticks on a foolish and unnecessary E and spells them *hause, pferde, hunde*. So, as an added E often signifies the plural, as the S does with us, the new student is likely to go on for a month making twins out of a Dative dog before he discovers his mistake; and on the other hand, many a new student who could ill afford loss, has bought and paid for two dogs and only got one of them, because he ignorantly bought that dog in the Dative singular when he really supposed he was talking plural—which left the law on the seller's side, of course, by the strict rules of grammar, and therefore a suit for recovery could not lie.

In German, all the Nouns begin with a capital letter. Now that is a good idea; and a good idea, in this language, is necessarily conspicuous from its lonesomeness. I consider this capitalizing of nouns a good idea, because by reason of it you are almost always able to tell a noun the minute you see it. You fall into error occasionally, because you mistake the name of a person for the name of a thing, and waste a good deal of time trying to dig a meaning out of it. German names almost always do mean something, and this helps to deceive the student. I translated a passage one day, which said that "the infuriated tigress broke loose and utterly ate up the unfortunate fir forest" (Tannenwald). When I was girding up my loins to doubt this, I found out that Tannenwald in this instance was a man's name.

13

Every noun has a gender, and there is no sense or system in the distribution; so the gender of each must be learned separately and by heart. There is no other way. To do this one has to have a memory like a memorandum-book. In German, a young lady has no sex, while a turnip has. Think what overwrought reverence that shows for the turnip, and what callous disrespect for the girl. See how it looks in print—I translate this from a conversation in one of the best of the German Sunday-school books:

"Gretchen. Wilhelm, where is the turnip?

"Wilhelm. She has gone to the kitchen.

"Gretchen. Where is the accomplished and beautiful English maiden?

"Wilhelm. It has gone to the opera."

To continue with the German genders: a tree is male, its buds are female, its leaves are neuter; horses are sexless, dogs are male, cats are female—tomcats included, of course; a person's mouth, neck, bosom, elbows, fingers, nails, feet, and body are of the male sex, and his head is male or neuter according to the word selected to signify it, and *not* according to the sex of the individual who wears it—for in Germany all the women wear either male heads or sexless ones; a person's nose, lips, shoulders, breast, hands, and toes are of the female sex; and his hair, ears, eyes, chin, legs, knees, heart, and conscience haven't any sex at all. The inventor of the language probably got what he knew about a conscience from hearsay.

Now, by the above dissection, the reader will see that in Germany a man may *think* he is a man, but when he comes to look into the matter closely, he is bound to have his doubts; he finds that in sober truth he is a most ridiculous mixture; and if he ends by trying to comfort himself with the thought that he can at least depend on a third of this mess as being manly and masculine, the humiliating second thought will quickly remind him that in this respect he is no better off than any woman or cow in the land.

14

In the German it is true that by some oversight of the inventor of the language, a Woman is a female; but a Wife (Weib) is not—which is unfortunate. A Wife, here, has no sex; she is neuter; so, according to the grammar, a fish is *he*, his scales are *she*, but a fishwife is neither. To describe a wife as sexless may be called under-description; that is bad enough, but over-description is surely worse. A German speaks of an Englishman as the *Englünnder*; to change the sex, he adds INN, and that stands for Englishwoman—*Englünderinn*. That seems descriptive enough, but still it is not exact enough for a German; so he precedes the word with that article which indicates that the creature to follow is feminine, and writes it down thus: "die Englünderinn,"—which means "the she-Englishwoman." I consider that that person is over-described.

Well, after the student has learned the sex of a great number of nouns, he is still in a difficulty, because he finds it impossible to persuade his tongue to refer to things as "he" and "she," and "him" and "her," which it has been always accustomed to refer to as "it." When he even frames a German sentence in his mind, with the hims and hers in the right places, and then works up his courage to the utterance-point, it is no use—the moment he begins to speak his tongue flies the track and all those labored males and females come out as "its." And even when he is reading German to himself, he always calls those things "it," whereas he ought to read in this way:

TALE OF THE FISHWIFE AND ITS SAD FATE [2]

It is a bleak Day. Hear the Rain, how he pours, and the Hail, how he rattles; and see the Snow, how he drifts along, and of the Mud, how deep he is! Ah the poor Fishwife, it is stuck fast in

2   I capitalize the nouns, in the German (and ancient English) fashion.

the Mire; it has dropped its Basket of Fishes; and its Hands have been cut by the Scales as it seized some of the falling Creatures; and one Scale has even got into its Eye, and it cannot get her out. It opens its Mouth to cry for Help; but if any Sound comes out of him, alas he is drowned by the raging of the Storm. And now a Tomcat has got one of the Fishes and she will surely escape with him. No, she bites off a Fin, she holds her in her Mouth—will she swallow her? No, the Fishwife's brave Mother-dog deserts his Puppies and rescues the Fin—which he eats, himself, as his Reward. O, horror, the Lightning has struck the Fish-basket; he sets him on Fire; see the Flame, how she licks the doomed Utensil with her red and angry Tongue; now she attacks the helpless Fishwife's Foot—she burns him up, all but the big Toe, and even *She* is partly consumed; and still she spreads, still she waves her fiery Tongues; she attacks the Fishwife's Leg and destroys *it*; she attacks its Hand and destroys *Her* also; she attacks the Fishwife's Leg and destroys *Her* also; she attacks its Body and consumes *Him*; she wreathes herself about its Heart and *it* is consumed; next about its Breast, and in a Moment *She* is a Cinder; now she reaches its Neck—He goes; now its Chin—*it* goes; now its Nose— *She* goes. In another Moment, except Help come, the Fishwife will be no more. Time presses—is there none to succor and save? Yes! Joy, joy, with flying Feet the she-Englishwoman comes! But alas, the generous she-Female is too late: where now is the fated Fishwife? It has ceased from its Sufferings, it has gone to a better Land; all that is left of it for its loved Ones to lament over, is this poor smoldering Ash-heap! Ah, woeful, woeful Ash-heap! Let us take him up tenderly, reverently, upon the lowly Shovel, and bear him to his long Rest, with the Prayer that when he rises again it will be a Realm where he will have one good square responsible Sex, and have it all to himself, instead of having a mangy lot of assorted Sexes scattered all over him in Spots.

There, now, the reader can see for himself that this pronoun business is a very awkward thing for the unaccustomed tongue. I suppose that in all languages the similarities of look and

sound between words which have no similarity in meaning
are a fruitful source of perplexity to the foreigner. It is so in
our tongue, and it is notably the case in the German. Now
there is that troublesome word *vermühlt*: to me it has so close
a resemblance—either real or fancied—to three or four other
words, that I never know whether it means despised, painted,
suspected, or married; until I look in the dictionary, and then I
find it means the latter. There are lots of such words and they are
a great torment. To increase the difficulty there are words which
seem to resemble each other, and yet do not; but they make just
as much trouble as if they did. For instance, there is the word
vermiethen (to let, to lease, to hire); and the word *verheirathen*
(another way of saying to marry). I heard of an Englishman who
knocked at a man's door in Heidelberg and proposed, in the
best German he could command, to "verheirathen" that house.
Then there are some words which mean one thing when you
emphasize the first syllable, but mean something very different
if you throw the emphasis on the last syllable. For instance,
there is a word which means a runaway, or the act of glancing
through a book, according to the placing of the emphasis; and
another word which signifies to *associate* with a man, or to *avoid*
him, according to where you put the emphasis—and you can
generally depend on putting it in the wrong place and getting
into trouble.

There are some exceedingly useful words in this language.
Schlag, for example; and *zug*. There are three-quarters of a
column of *schlags* in the dictonary, and a column and a half of
zugs. The word *schlag* means Blow, Stroke, Dash, Hit, Shock,
Clap, Slap, Time, Bar, Coin, Stamp, Kind, Sort, Manner, Way,
Apoplexy, Wood-cutting, Enclosure, Field, Forest-clearing. This
is its simple and *exact* meaning—that is to say, its restricted, its
fettered meaning; but there are ways by which you can set it free,
so that it can soar away, as on the wings of the morning, and
never be at rest. You can hang any word you please to its tail,
and make it mean anything you want to. You can begin with

schlag-ader, which means artery, and you can hang on the whole dictionary, word by word, clear through the alphabet to *schlag-wasser*, which means bilge-water—and including *schlag-mutte*R, which means mother-in-law.

Just the same with *zug*. Strictly speaking, *zug* means Pull, Tug, Draught, Procession, March, Progress, Flight, Direction, Expedition, Train, Caravan, Passage, Stroke, Touch, Line, Flourish, Trait of Character, Feature, Lineament, Chess-move, Organ-stop, Team, Whiff, Bias, Drawer, Propensity, Inhalation, Disposition: but that thing which it does *not* mean—when all its legitimate pennants have been hung on, has not been discovered yet.

One cannot overestimate the usefulness of *schlag* and *zug*. Armed just with these two, and the word *also*, what cannot the foreigner on German soil accomplish? The German word *also* is the equivalent of the English phrase "You know," and does not mean anything at all—in *talk*, though it sometimes does in print. Every time a German opens his mouth an *also* falls out; and every time he shuts it he bites one in two that was trying to *get* out.

Now, the foreigner, equipped with these three noble words, is master of the situation. Let him talk right along, fearlessly; let him pour his indifferent German forth, and when he lacks for a word, let him heave a *schlag* into the vacuum; all the chances are that it fits it like a plug, but if it doesn't let him promptly heave a *zug* after it; the two together can hardly fail to bung the hole; but if, by a miracle, they *should* fail, let him simply say *also*! and this will give him a moment's chance to think of the needful word. In Germany, when you load your conversational gun it is always best to throw in a *schlag* or two and a *zug* or two, because it doesn't make any difference how much the rest of the charge may scatter, you are bound to bag something with *them*. Then you blandly say *also*, and load up again. Nothing gives such an air of grace and elegance and unconstraint to a German or an English conversation as to scatter it full of

18

"Also's" or "You knows."

In my note-book I find this entry:

> July 1.—In the hospital yesterday, a word of thirteen syllables was successfully removed from a patient—a North German from near Hamburg; but as most unfortunately the surgeons had opened him in the wrong place, under the impression that he contained a panorama, he died. The sad event has cast a gloom over the whole community.

That paragraph furnishes a text for a few remarks about one of the most curious and notable features of my subject—the length of German words. Some German words are so long that they have a perspective. Observe these examples:

Freundschaftsbezeigungen.
Dilettantenaufdringlichkeiten.
Stadtverordnetenversammlungen.

These things are not words, they are alphabetical processions. And they are not rare; one can open a German newspaper at any time and see them marching majestically across the page— and if he has any imagination he can see the banners and hear the music, too. They impart a martial thrill to the meekest subject. I take a great interest in these curiosities. Whenever I come across a good one, I stuff it and put it in my museum. In this way I have made quite a valuable collection. When I get duplicates, I exchange with other collectors, and thus increase the variety of my stock. Here are some specimens which I lately bought at an auction sale of the effects of a bankrupt bric-a-brac hunter:

GENERALSTAATSVERORDNETENVERSAMMLUNGEN.
ALTERTHUMSWISSENSCHAFTEN.
KINDERBEWAHRUNGSANSTALTEN.
UNABHÄNGIGKEITSERKLÄRUNGEN.
WIEDERERSTELLUNGBESTREBUNGEN.
WAFFENSTILLSTANDSUNTERHANDLUNGEN.

Of course when one of these grand mountain ranges goes stretching across the printed page, it adorns and ennobles that literary landscape—but at the same time it is a great distress to the new student, for it blocks up his way; he cannot crawl under it, or climb over it, or tunnel through it. So he resorts to the dictionary for help, but there is no help there. The dictionary must draw the line somewhere—so it leaves this sort of words out. And it is right, because these long things are hardly legitimate words, but are rather combinations of words, and the inventor of them ought to have been killed. They are compound words with the hyphens left out. The various words used in building them are in the dictionary, but in a very scattered condition; so you can hunt the materials out, one by one, and get at the meaning at last, but it is a tedious and harassing business. I have tried this process upon some of the above examples. "Freundshaftsbezeigungen" seems to be "Friendship demonstrations," which is only a foolish and clumsy way of saying "demonstrations of friendship." "Unabhängigkeitserklärungen" seems to be "Independencedeclarations," which is no improvement upon "Declarations of Independence," so far as I can see. "Generalstaatsverordnetenversammlungen" seems to be "General-statesrepresentativesmeetings," as nearly as I can get at it—a mere rhythmical, gushy euphemism for "meetings of the legislature," I judge. We used to have a good deal of this sort of crime in our literature, but it has gone out now. We used to speak of a thing as a "never-to-be-forgotten" circumstance, instead of cramping it into the simple and sufficient word

20

"memorable" and then going calmly about our business as if nothing had happened. In those days we were not content to embalm the thing and bury it decently, we wanted to build a monument over it.

But in our newspapers the compounding-disease lingers a little to the present day, but with the hyphens left out, in the German fashion. This is the shape it takes: instead of saying "Mr. Simmons, clerk of the county and district courts, was in town yesterday," the new form puts it thus: "Clerk of the County and District Courts Simmons was in town yesterday." This saves neither time nor ink, and has an awkward sound besides. One often sees a remark like this in our papers: "*Mrs.* Assistant District Attorney Johnson returned to her city residence yesterday for the season." That is a case of really unjustifiable compounding; because it not only saves no time or trouble, but confers a title on Mrs. Johnson which she has no right to. But these little instances are trifles indeed, contrasted with the ponderous and dismal German system of piling jumbled compounds together. I wish to submit the following local item, from a Mannheim journal, by way of illustration:

"In the daybeforeyesterdayshortlyaftereleveno'clock Night, the inthistownstandingtavern called 'The Wagoner' was downburnt. When the fire to the onthedownburninghouseresting Stork's Nest reached, flew the parent Storks away. But when the byteraging, firesurrounded Nest *itself* caught Fire, straightway plunged the quickreturning Mother-Stork into the Flames and died, her Wings over her young ones outspread."

Even the cumbersome German construction is not able to take the pathos out of that picture—indeed, it somehow seems to strengthen it. This item is dated away back yonder months ago. I could have used it sooner, but I was waiting to hear from the Father-stork. I am still waiting.

"*Also!*" If I had not shown that the German is a difficult language, I have at least intended to do so. I have heard of an American student who was asked how he was getting along with his German, and who answered promptly: "I am not getting along at all. I have worked at it hard for three level months, and all I have got to show for it is one solitary German phrase— '*zwei glas*'" (two glasses of beer). He paused for a moment, reflectively; then added with feeling: "But I've got that *solid!*"

And if I have not also shown that German is a harassing and infuriating study, my execution has been at fault, and not my intent. I heard lately of a worn and sorely tried American student who used to fly to a certain German word for relief when he could bear up under his aggravations no longer— the only word whose sound was sweet and precious to his ear and healing to his lacerated spirit. This was the word *damit*. It was only the *sound* that helped him, not the meaning; [3] and so, at last, when he learned that the emphasis was not on the first syllable, his only stay and support was gone, and he faded away and died.

I think that a description of any loud, stirring, tumultuous episode must be tamer in German than in English. Our descriptive words of this character have such a deep, strong, resonant sound, while their German equivalents do seem so thin and mild and energyless. Boom, burst, crash, roar, storm, bellow, blow, thunder, explosion; howl, cry, shout, yell, groan; battle, hell. These are magnificent words; the have a force and magnitude of sound befitting the things which they describe. But their German equivalents would be ever so nice to sing the children to sleep with, or else my awe-inspiring ears were made for display and not for superior usefulness in analyzing sounds. Would any man want to die in a battle which was called by so tame a term as a *schlacht*? Or would not a comsumptive feel too much bundled up, who was about to go out, in a shirt-collar and a seal-ring, into a storm which the bird-song word *gewitter* was employed to describe? And observe the strongest of the several German equivalents for explosion—*ausbruch*. Our word

---

3   It merely means, in its general sense, "*herewith*."

Toothbrush is more powerful than that. It seems to me that the Germans could do worse than import it into their language to describe particularly tremendous explosions with. The German word for hell—Hoelle—sounds more like *helly* than anything else; therefore, how necessarily chipper, frivolous, and unimpressive it is. If a man were told in German to go there, could he really rise to thee dignity of feeling insulted?

Having pointed out, in detail, the several vices of this language, I now come to the brief and pleasant task of pointing out its virtues. The capitalizing of the nouns I have already mentioned. But far before this virtue stands another—that of spelling a word according to the sound of it. After one short lesson in the alphabet, the student can tell how any German word is pronounced without having to ask; whereas in our language if a student should inquire of us, "What does B, O, W, spell?" we should be obliged to reply, "Nobody can tell what it spells when you set if off by itself; you can only tell by referring to the context and finding out what it signifies—whether it is a thing to shoot arrows with, or a nod of one's head, or the forward end of a boat."

There are some German words which are singularly and powerfully effective. For instance, those which describe lowly, peaceful, and affectionate home life; those which deal with love, in any and all forms, from mere kindly feeling and honest good will toward the passing stranger, clear up to courtship; those which deal with outdoor Nature, in its softest and loveliest aspects—with meadows and forests, and birds and flowers, the fragrance and sunshine of summer, and the moonlight of peaceful winter nights; in a word, those which deal with any and all forms of rest, repose, and peace; those also which deal with the creatures and marvels of fairyland; and lastly and chiefly, in those words which express pathos, is the language surpassingly rich and affective. There are German songs which can make a stranger to the language cry. That shows that the *sound* of the words is correct—it interprets the meanings with truth and with exactness; and so the ear is informed, and through the ear, the heart.

The Germans do not seem to be afraid to repeat a word when it is the right one. They repeat it several times, if they choose. That is wise. But in English, when we have used a word a couple of times in a paragraph, we imagine we are growing tautological, and so we are weak enough to exchange it for some other word which only approximates exactness, to escape what we wrongly fancy is a greater blemish. Repetition may be bad, but surely inexactness is worse.

There are people in the world who will take a great deal of trouble to point out the faults in a religion or a language, and then go blandly about their business without suggesting any remedy. I am not that kind of person. I have shown that the German language needs reforming. Very well, I am ready to reform it. At least I am ready to make the proper suggestions. Such a course as this might be immodest in another; but I have devoted upward of nine full weeks, first and last, to a careful and critical study of this tongue, and thus have acquired a confidence in my ability to reform it which no mere superficial culture could have conferred upon me.

In the first place, I would leave out the Dative case. It confuses the plurals; and, besides, nobody ever knows when he is in the Dative case, except he discover it by accident—and then he does not know when or where it was that he got into it, or how long he has been in it, or how he is ever going to get out of it again. The Dative case is but an ornamental folly—it is better to discard it.

In the next place, I would move the Verb further up to the front. You may load up with ever so good a Verb, but I notice that you never really bring down a subject with it at the present German range—you only cripple it. So I insist that this important part of speech should be brought forward to a position where it may be easily seen with the naked eye.

Thirdly, I would import some strong words from the English tongue—to swear with, and also to use in describing all sorts of vigorous things in a vigorous way. [4]

Fourthly, I would reorganizes the sexes, and distribute them accordingly to the will of the creator. This as a tribute of respect, if nothing else.

Fifthly, I would do away with those great long compounded words; or require the speaker to deliver them in sections, with intermissions for refreshments. To wholly do away with them would be best, for ideas are more easily received and digested when they come one at a time than when they come in bulk. Intellectual food is like any other; it is pleasanter and more beneficial to take it with a spoon than with a shovel.

Sixthly, I would require a speaker to stop when he is done, and not hang a string of those useless "haven sind gewesen gehabt haben geworden seins" to the end of his oration. This sort of gewgaws undignify a speech, instead of adding a grace. They are, therefore, an offense, and should be discarded.

Seventhly, I would discard the Parenthesis. Also the reparenthesis, the re-reparenthesis, and the re-re-re-re-re-reparentheses, and likewise the final wide-reaching all-enclosing king-parenthesis. I would require every individual, be he high or low, to unfold a plain straightforward tale, or else coil it and

---

4   "Verdammt," and its variations and enlargements, are words which have plenty of meaning, but the *sounds* are so mild and ineffectual that German ladies can use them without sin. German ladies who could not be induced to commit a sin by any persuasion or compulsion, promptly rip out one of these harmless little words when they tear their dresses or don't like the soup. It sounds about as wicked as our "My gracious." German ladies are constantly saying, "Ach! Gott!" "Mein Gott!" "Gott in Himmel!" "Herr Gott" "Der Herr Jesus!" etc. They think our ladies have the same custom, perhaps; for I once heard a gentle and lovely old German lady say to a sweet young American girl: "The two languages are so alike—how pleasant that is; we say 'Ach! Gott!' you say 'Goddamn.'"

sit on it and hold his peace. Infractions of this law should be punishable with death.

And eighthly, and last, I would retain *zug* and *schlag*, with their pendants, and discard the rest of the vocabulary. This would simplify the language.

I have now named what I regard as the most necessary and important changes. These are perhaps all I could be expected to name for nothing; but there are other suggestions which I can and will make in case my proposed application shall result in my being formally employed by the government in the work of reforming the language.

My philological studies have satisfied me that a gifted person ought to learn English (barring spelling and pronouncing) in thirty hours, French in thirty days, and German in thirty years. It seems manifest, then, that the latter tongue ought to be trimmed down and repaired. If it is to remain as it is, it ought to be gently and reverently set aside among the dead languages, for only the dead have time to learn it.

A FOURTH OF JULY
ORATION IN THE GERMAN TONGUE,
Delivered at a Banquet of the
Anglo-American Club of Students
by the Author of this Book

GENTLEMEN: Since I arrived, a month ago, in this old wonderland, this vast garden of Germany, my English tongue has so often proved a useless piece of baggage to me, and so troublesome to carry around, in a country where they haven't the checking system for luggage, that I finally set to work, and learned the German language. Also! Es freut mich dass dies so ist, denn es muss, in ein hauptsächlich degree, höflich sein, dass man auf ein occasion like this, sein Rede in die Sprache des Landes worin he boards, aussprechen soll. Dafuer habe ich, aus reinische Verlegenheit—no, Vergangenheit—no, I mean Höflichkeit—aus reinishe Höflichkeit habe ich resolved to tackle this business in the German language, um Gottes willen! Also! Sie muessen so freundlich sein, und verzeih mich die interlarding von ein oder zwei Englischer Worte, hie und da, denn ich finde dass die deutsche is not a very copious language, and so when you've really got anything to say, you've got to draw on a language that can stand the strain.

Wenn haber man kann nicht meinem Rede Verstehen, so werde ich ihm später dasselbe uebersetz, wenn er solche Dienst verlangen wollen haben werden sollen sein hätte. (I don't know what wollen haben werden sollen sein hätte means, but I notice they always put it at the end of a German sentence—merely for general literary gorgeousness, I suppose.)

This is a great and justly honored day—a day which is worthy of the veneration in which it is held by the true patriots of all climes and nationalities—a day which offers a fruitful theme for thought and speech; und meinem Freunde—no, meinen Freunden—meines Freundes—well, take your choice, they're all the same price; I don't know which one is right—also! ich habe gehabt haben worden gewesen sein, as Goethe says in his Paradise Lost—ich—ich—that is to say—ich—but let us change cars.

Also! Die Anblich so viele Grossbrittanischer und Amerikanischer hier zusammengetroffen in Bruderliche concord, ist zwar a welcome and inspiriting spectacle.

And what has moved you to it?

Can the terse German tongue rise to the expression of this impulse?

Is it Freundschaftsbezeigungenstadtverordnetenversammlu ngenfamilieneigenthümlichkeiten? Nein, O nein! This is a crisp and noble word, but it fails to pierce the marrow of the impulse which has gathered this friendly meeting and produced diese Anblick—eine Anblich welche ist gut zu sehen—gut fuer die Augen in a foreign land and a far country—eine Anblick solche als in die gewöhnliche Heidelberger phrase nennt man ein "schönes Aussicht!" Ja, freilich natürlich wahrscheinlich ebensowohl! Also! Die Aussicht auf dem Koenigsstuhl mehr grösser ist, aber geistlische sprechend nicht so schön, lob' Gott! Because sie sind hier zusammengetroffen, in Bruderlichem concord, ein grossen Tag zu feirn, whose high benefits were not for one land and one locality, but have conferred a measure of good upon all lands that know liberty today, and love it. Hundert Jahre vorueber, waren die Engländer und die Amerikaner Feinde; aber heut sind sie herzlichen Freunde, Gott sei Dank! May this good-fellowship endure; may these banners here blended in amity so remain; may they never any more wave over opposing hosts, or be stained with blood which was kindred, is kindred, and always will be kindred, until a line drawn upon a map shall be able to say: "*This* bars the ancestral blood from flowing in the veins of the descendant!"

First published in 1880 as
Appendix D in *A Tramp Abroad.*

HOW TO TELL A STORY

The Humorous Story, an American Development.—
Its Difference from Comic and Witty Stories

I do not claim that I can tell a story as it ought to be told. I only claim to know how a story ought to be told, for I have been almost daily in the company of the most expert story-tellers for many years.

There are several kinds of stories, but only one difficult kind—the humorous. I will talk mainly about that one. The humorous story is American, the comic story is English, the witty story is French. The humorous story depends for its effect upon the manner of the telling; the comic story and the witty story upon the matter.

The humorous story may be spun out to great length, and may wander around as much as it pleases, and arrive nowhere in particular; but the comic and witty stories must be brief and end with a point. The humorous story bubbles gently along, the others burst.

The humorous story is strictly a work of art—high and delicate art—and only an artist can tell it; but no art is necessary in telling the comic and the witty story; anybody can do it. The art of telling a humorous story—understand, I mean by word of mouth, not print—was created in America, and has remained at home.

The humorous story is told gravely; the teller does his best to conceal the fact that he even dimly suspects that there is anything funny about it; but the teller of the comic story tells you beforehand that it is one of the funniest things he has ever heard, then tells it with eager delight, and is the first person to laugh when he gets through. And sometimes, if he has had good success, he is so glad and happy that he will repeat the "nub" of it and glance around from face to face, collecting applause, and then repeat it again. It is a pathetic thing to see.

Very often, of course, the rambling and disjointed humorous story finishes with a nub, point, snapper, or whatever you like to call it. Then the listener must be alert, for in many cases the teller will divert attention from that nub by dropping it in a carefully casual and indifferent way, with the pretence that he does not know it is a nub.

Artemus Ward used that trick a good deal; then when the belated audience presently caught the joke he would look up with innocent surprise, as if wondering what they had found to laugh at. Dan Setchell used it before him, Nye and Riley and others use it to-day.

But the teller of the comic story does not slur the nub; he shouts it at you—every time. And when he prints it, in England, France, Germany, and Italy, he italicizes it, puts some whooping exclamation-points after it, and sometimes explains it in a parenthesis. All of which is very depressing, and makes one want to renounce joking and lead a better life.

Let me set down an instance of the comic method, using an anecdote which has been popular all over the world for twelve or fifteen hundred years. The teller tells it in this way:

THE WOUNDED SOLDIER

In the course of a certain battle a soldier whose leg had been shot off appealed to another soldier who was hurrying by to carry him to the rear, informing him at the same time of the loss which he had sustained; whereupon the generous son of Mars, shouldering the unfortunate, proceeded to carry out his desire. The bullets and cannon-balls were flying in all directions, and

presently one of the latter took the wounded man's head off—
without, however, his deliverer being aware of it. In no-long
time he was hailed by an officer, who said:

"Where are you going with that carcass?"

"To the rear, sir—he's lost his leg!"

"His leg, forsooth?" responded the astonished officer; "you
mean his head, you booby."

Whereupon the soldier dispossessed himself of his burden,
and stood looking down upon it in great perplexity. At
length he said:

"It is true, sir, just as you have said." Then after a pause he
added, "But he TOLD me IT WAS HIS LEG—"

Here the narrator bursts into explosion after explosion of
thunderous horse-laughter, repeating that nub from time to
time through his gaspings and shriekings and suffocatings.

It takes only a minute and a half to tell that in its comic-story
form; and isn't worth the telling, after all. Put into the humorous-
story form it takes ten minutes, and is about the funniest thing I
have ever listened to—as James Whitcomb Riley tells it.

He tells it in the character of a dull-witted old farmer who has
just heard it for the first time, thinks it is unspeakably funny,
and is trying to repeat it to a neighbor. But he can't remember it;
so he gets all mixed up and wanders helplessly round and round,
putting in tedious details that don't belong in the tale and only
retard it; taking them out conscientiously and putting in others
that are just as useless; making minor mistakes now and then
and stopping to correct them and explain how he came to make
them; remembering things which he forgot to put in in their
proper place and going back to put them in there; stopping his
narrative a good while in order to try to recall the name of the
soldier that was hurt, and finally remembering that the soldier's
name was not mentioned, and remarking placidly that the name
is of no real importance, anyway—better, of course, if one knew
it, but not essential, after all—and so on, and so on, and so on.

The teller is innocent and happy and pleased with himself,

and has to stop every little while to hold himself in and keep from laughing outright; and does hold in, but his body quakes in a jelly-like way with interior chuckles; and at the end of the ten minutes the audience have laughed until they are exhausted, and the tears are running down their faces.

The simplicity and innocence and sincerity and unconsciousness of the old farmer are perfectly simulated, and the result is a performance which is thoroughly charming and delicious. This is art and fine and beautiful, and only a master can compass it; but a machine could tell the other story.

To string incongruities and absurdities together in a wandering and sometimes purposeless way, and seem innocently unaware that they are absurdities, is the basis of the American art, if my position is correct. Another feature is the slurring of the point. A third is the dropping of a studied remark apparently without knowing it, as if one were thinking aloud. The fourth and last is the pause.

Artemus Ward dealt in numbers three and four a good deal. He would begin to tell with great animation something which he seemed to think was wonderful; then lose confidence, and after an apparently absent-minded pause add an incongruous remark in a soliloquizing way; and that was the remark intended to explode the mine—and it did.

For instance, he would say eagerly, excitedly, "I once knew a man in New Zealand who hadn't a tooth in his head"—here his animation would die out; a silent, reflective pause would follow, then he would say dreamily, and as if to himself, "and yet that man could beat a drum better than any man I ever saw."

The pause is an exceedingly important feature in any kind of story, and a frequently recurring feature, too. It is a dainty thing, and delicate, and also uncertain and treacherous; for it must be exactly the right length—no more and no less—or it fails of its purpose and makes trouble. If the pause is too short the impressive point is passed, and [and if too long] the audience have had time to divine that a surprise is intended—and then you can't surprise them, of course.

On the platform I used to tell a negro ghost story that had a pause in front of the snapper on the end, and that pause was the most important thing in the whole story. If I got it the right length precisely, I could spring the finishing ejaculation with effect enough to make some impressible girl deliver a startled little yelp and jump out of her seat—and that was what I was after. This story was called "The Golden Arm," and was told in this fashion. You can practise with it yourself—and mind you look out for the pause and get it right.

THE GOLDEN ARM

Once 'pon a time dey wuz a monsus mean man, en he live 'way out in de prairie all 'lone by hisself, 'cep'n he had a wife. En bimeby she died, en he tuck en toted her way out dah in de prairie en buried her. Well, she had a golden arm—all solid gold, fum de shoulder down. He wuz pow'ful mean—pow'ful; en dat night he couldn't sleep, Gaze he want dat golden arm so bad.

When it come midnight he couldn't stan' it no mo'; so he git up, he did, en tuck his lantern en shoved out thoo de storm en dug her up en got de golden arm; en he bent his head down 'gin de win', en plowed en plowed en plowed thoo de snow. Den all on a sudden he stop (make a considerable pause here, and look startled, and take a listening attitude) en say: "My LAN', what's dat!"

En he listen—en listen—en de win' say (set your teeth together and imitate the wailing and wheezing singsong of the wind), "Bzzz-z-zzz"—en den, way back yonder whah de grave is, he hear a voice! he hear a voice all mix' up in de win' can't hardly tell 'em 'part—"Bzzz-zzz—W-h-o—g-o-t—m-y—g-o-l-d-e-n arm?—zzz—zzz—W-h-o g-o-t m-y g-o-l-d-e-n arm!" (You must begin to shiver violently now.)

En he begin to shiver en shake, en say, "Oh, my! OH, my lan'!"

en de win' blow de lantern out, en de snow en sleet blow in his face en mos' choke him, en he start a-plowin' knee-deep towards home mos' dead, he so sk'yerd—en pooty soon he hear de voice agin, en (pause) it 'us comin' after him! "Bzzz—zzz—zzz—W-h-o—g-o-t m-y—g-o-l-d-e-n—arm?"

When he git to de pasture he hear it agin closter now, en a-comin'!—a-comin' back dah in de dark en de storm—(repeat the wind and the voice). When he git to de house he rush up-stairs en jump in de bed en kiver up, head and years, en lay dah shiverin' en shakin'—en den way out dah he hear it agin!—en a-comin'! En bimeby he hear (pause—awed, listening attitude)—pat—pat—pat—hit's acomin' up-stairs! Den he hear de latch, en he know it's in de room!

Den pooty soon he know it's a-stannin' by de bed! (Pause.) Den—he know it's a-bendin' down over him—en he cain't skasely git his breath! Den—den—he seem to feel someth' n c-o-l-d, right down 'most agin his head! (Pause.)

Den de voice say, right at his year—"W-h-o g-o-t—m-y—g-o-l-d-e-n arm?" (You must wail it out very plaintively and accusingly; then you stare steadily and impressively into the face of the farthest-gone auditor—a girl, preferably—and let that awe-inspiring pause begin to build itself in the deep hush. When it has reached exactly the right length, jump suddenly at that girl and yell, "You've got it!")

If you've got the pause right, she'll fetch a dear little yelp and spring right out of her shoes. But you must get the pause right; and you will find it the most troublesome and aggravating and uncertain thing you ever undertook.

First published in 1897.

ADVICE TO YOUTH

Being told I would be expected to talk here, I inquired what sort of talk I ought to make. They said it should be something suitable to youth-something didactic, instructive, or something in the nature of good advice. Very well. I have a few things in my mind which I have often longed to say for the instruction of the young; for it is in one's tender early years that such things will best take root and be most enduring and most valuable. First, then. I will say to you my young friends — and I say it beseechingly, urgently — Always obey your parents, when they are present. This is the best policy in the long run, because if you don't, they will make you. Most parents think they know better than you do, and you can generally make more by humoring that superstition than you can by acting on your own better judgment

Be respectful to your superiors, if you have any, also to strangers, and sometimes to others. If a person offend you, and you are in doubt as to whether it was intentional or not, do not resort to extreme measures; simply watch your chance and hit him with a brick. That will be sufficient. If you shall find that he had not intended any offense, come out frankly and confess yourself in the wrong when you struck him; acknowledge it like a man and say you didn't mean to. Yes, always avoid violence; in this age of charity and kindliness, the time has gone by for such things. Leave dynamite to the low and unrefined.

Go to bed early, get up early — this is wise. Some authorities say get up with the sun; some say get up with one thing, others with another. But a lark is really the best thing to get up with. It gives you a splendid reputation with everybody to know that you get up with the lark; and if you get the right kind of lark, and work at him right, you can easily train him to get up at half past nine, every time — it's no trick at all.

Now as to the matter of lying. You want to be very careful about lying; otherwise you are nearly sure to get caught. Once caught, you can never again be in the eyes to the good and the pure, what you were before. Many a young person has injured himself permanently through a single clumsy and ill finished lie, the result of carelessness born of incomplete training. Some authorities hold that the young out not to lie at all. That of course, is putting it rather stronger than necessary; still while I cannot go quite so far as that, I do maintain , and I believe I am right, that the young ought to be temperate in the use of this great art until practice and experience shall give them that confidence, elegance, and precision which alone can make the accomplishment graceful and profitable. Patience, diligence, painstaking attention to detail — these are requirements; these in time, will make the student perfect; upon these only, may he rely as the sure foundation for future eminence. Think what tedious years of study, thought, practice, experience, went to the equipment of that peerless old master who was able to impose upon the whole world the lofty and sounding maxim that "Truth is mighty and will prevail" — the most majestic compound fracture of fact which any of woman born has yet achieved. For the history of our race, and each individual's experience, are sewn thick with evidences that a truth is not hard to kill, and that a lie well told is immortal. There is in Boston a monument of the man who discovered anesthesia; many people are aware, in these latter days, that that man didn't discover it at all, but stole the discovery from another man. Is this truth mighty, and will it prevail? Ah no, my hearers, the monument is made of hardy material, but the lie it tells will outlast it a million years. An awkward, feeble, leaky lie is a thing which you ought to make it your unceasing study to avoid; such a lie as that has no more real permanence than an average truth. Why, you might as well tell the truth at once and be done with it. A feeble, stupid, preposterous lie will not live two years — except it be a slander upon somebody. It is indestructible, then of course, but that is no merit of yours. A final word: begin your practice of this gracious and beautiful art early — begin now. If I had begun earlier, I could have learned how.

Never handle firearms carelessly. The sorrow and suffering that have been caused through the innocent but heedless handling of firearms by the young! Only four days ago, right in the next farm house to the one where I am spending the summer, a grandmother, old and gray and sweet, one of the loveliest spirits in the land, was sitting at her work, when her young grandson crept in and got down an old, battered, rusty gun which had not been touched for many years and was supposed not to be loaded, and pointed it at her, laughing and threatening to shoot. In her fright she ran screaming and pleading toward the door on the other side of the room; but as she passed him he placed the gun almost against her very breast and pulled the trigger! He had supposed it was not loaded. And he was right — it wasn't. So there wasn't any harm done. It is the only case of that kind I ever heard of. Therefore, just the same, don't you meddle with old unloaded firearms; they are the most deadly and unerring hings that have ever been created by man. You don't have to take any pains at all with them; you don't have to have a rest, you don't have to have any sights on the gun, you don't have to take aim, even. No, you just pick out a relative and bang away, and you are sure to get him. A youth who can't hit a cathedral at thirty yards with a Gatling gun in three quarters of an hour, can take up an old empty musket and bag his grandmother every time, at a hundred. Think what Waterloo would have been if one of the armies had been boys armed with old muskets supposed not to be loaded, and the other army had been composed of their female relations. The very thought of it make one shudder.

There are many sorts of books; but good ones are the sort for the young to read. remember that. They are a great, an inestimable, and unspeakable means of improvement. Therefore be careful in your selection, my young friends; be very careful; confine yourselves exclusively to Robertson's *Sermons*, Baxter's *Saints' Rest*, *The Innocents Abroad*, and works of that kind.

But I have said enough. I hope you will treasure up the instructions which I have given you, and make them a guide to your feet and a light to your understanding. Build your character thoughtfully and painstakingly upon these precepts, and by and by, when you have got it built, you will be surprised and gratified to see how nicely and sharply it resembles everybody else's.

First published in 1882.

TAMING THE BICYCLE

I thought the matter over, and concluded I could do it. So I went down and bought a barrel of Pond's Extract and a bicycle. The Expert came home with me to instruct me. We chose the back yard, for the sake of privacy, and went to work.

Mine was not a full-grown bicycle, but only a colt—a fifty-inch, with the pedals shortened up to forty-eight—and skittish, like any other colt. The Expert explained the thing's points briefly, then he got on its back and rode around a little, to show me how easy it was to do. He said that the dismounting was perhaps the hardest thing to learn, and so we would leave that to the last. But he was in error there. He found, to his surprise and joy, that all that he needed to do was to get me on to the machine and stand out of the way; I could get off, myself. Although I was wholly inexperienced, I dismounted in the best time on record. He was on that side, shoving up the machine; we all came down with a crash, he at the bottom, I next, and the machine on top.

We examined the machine, but it was not in the least injured. This was hardly believable. Yet the Expert assured me that it was true; in fact, the examination proved it. I was partly to realize, then, how admirably these things are constructed. We applied some Pond's Extract, and resumed. The Expert got on the *other* side to shove up this time, but I dismounted on that side; so the result was as before.

The machine was not hurt. We oiled ourselves up again, and resumed. This time the Expert took up a sheltered position behind, but somehow or other we landed on him again.

He was full of surprised admiration; said it was abnormal. She was all right, not a scratch on her, not a timber started anywhere. I said it was wonderful, while we were greasing up, but he said that when I came to know these steel spider-webs I would realize that nothing but dynamite could cripple them. Then he limped out to position, and we resumed once more. This time the Expert took up the position of short-stop, and got a man to shove up behind. We got up a handsome speed, and presently traversed a brick, and I went out over the top of the tiller and landed, head down, on the instructor's back, and saw the machine fluttering in the air between me and the sun. It was well it came down on us, for that broke the fall, and it was not injured.

Five days later I got out and was carried down to the hospital, and found the Expert doing pretty fairly. In a few more days I was quite sound. I attribute this to my prudence in always dismounting on something soft. Some recommend a feather bed, but I think an Expert is better.

The Expert got out at last, brought four assistants with him. It was a good idea. These four held the graceful cobweb upright while I climbed into the saddle; then they formed in column and marched on either side of me while the Expert pushed behind; all hands assisted at the dismount.

The bicycle had what is called the "wabbles," and had them very badly. In order to keep my position, a good many things were required of me, and in every instance the thing required was against nature. Against nature, but not against the laws of nature. That is to say, that whatever the needed thing might be, my nature, habit, and breeding moved me to attempt it in one way, while some immutable and unsuspected law of physics required that it be done in just the other way. I perceived by this how radically and grotesquely wrong had been the life-long education of my body and members. They were steeped in ignorance; they knew nothing—nothing which it could profit them to know. For instance, if I found myself falling to the right, I put the tiller hard down the other way, by a quite natural impulse, and so violated a law, and kept on going down. The law required the opposite thing—the big wheel must be turned in the direction in which you are falling. It is hard to believe this, when you are told it. And not merely hard to believe it, but impossible; it is opposed to all your notions. And it is just as hard to do it, after you do come to believe it. Believing it, and knowing by the most convincing proof that it is true, does not help it: you can't any more DO it than you could before; you can neither force nor persuade yourself to do it at first. The intellect has to come to the front, now. It has to teach the limbs to discard their old education and adopt the new.

The steps of one's progress are distinctly marked. At the end of each lesson he knows he has acquired something, and he also knows what that something is, and likewise that it will stay with him. It is not like studying German, where you mull along, in a groping, uncertain way, for thirty years; and at last, just as you think you've got it, they spring the subjunctive on you, and there you are. No—and I see now, plainly enough, that the great pity about the German language is, that you can't fall off it and hurt yourself. There is nothing like that feature to make you attend strictly to business. But I also see, by what I have learned of bicycling, that the right and only sure way to learn German is by the bicycling method. That is to say, take a grip on one villainy of it at a time, and learn it—not ease up and shirk to the next, leaving that one half learned.

When you have reached the point in bicycling where you can balance the machine tolerably fairly and propel it and steer it, then comes your next task—how to mount it. You do it in this way: you hop along behind it on your right foot, resting the other on the mounting-peg, and grasping the tiller with your hands. At the word, you rise on the peg, stiffen your left leg, hang your other one around in the air in a general in indefinite way, lean your stomach against the rear of the saddle, and then fall off, maybe on one side, maybe on the other; but you fall off. You get up and do it again; and once more; and then several times.

By this time you have learned to keep your balance; and also to steer without wrenching the tiller out by the roots (I say tiller because it IS a tiller; "handle-bar" is a lamely descriptive phrase). So you steer along, straight ahead, a little while, then you rise forward, with a steady strain, bringing your right leg, and then your body, into the saddle, catch your breath, fetch a violent hitch this way and then that, and down you go again.

But you have ceased to mind the going down by this time; you are getting to light on one foot or the other with considerable certainty. Six more attempts and six more falls make you perfect. You land in the saddle comfortably, next time, and stay there— that is, if you can be content to let your legs dangle, and leave the pedals alone a while; but if you grab at once for the pedals, you are gone again. You soon learn to wait a little and perfect your balance before reaching for the pedals; then the mounting-art is acquired, is complete, and a little practice will make it simple and easy to you, though spectators ought to keep off a rod or two to one side, along at first, if you have nothing against them.

And now you come to the voluntary dismount; you learned the other kind first of all. It is quite easy to tell one how to do the voluntary dismount; the words are few, the requirement simple, and apparently undifficult; let your left pedal go down till your left leg is nearly straight, turn your wheel to the left, and get off as you would from a horse. It certainly does sound exceedingly easy; but it isn't. I don't know why it isn't but it isn't. Try as you may, you don't get down as you would from a horse, you get down as you would from a house afire. You make a spectacle of yourself every time.

II

During the eight days I took a daily lesson of an hour and a half. At the end of this twelve working-hours' apprenticeship I was graduated—in the rough. I was pronounced competent to paddle my own bicycle without outside help. It seems incredible, this celerity of acquirement. It takes considerably longer than that to learn horseback-riding in the rough.

Now it is true that I could have learned without a teacher, but it would have been risky for me, because of my natural clumsiness. The self-taught man seldom knows anything accurately, and he does not know a tenth as much as he could have known if he had worked under teachers; and, besides, he brags, and is the means of fooling other thoughtless people into going and doing as he himself has done. There are those who imagine that the unlucky accidents of life—life's "experiences"—are in some way useful to us. I wish I could find out how. I never knew one of them to happen twice. They always change off and swap around and catch you on your inexperienced side. If personal experience can be worth anything as an education, it wouldn't seem likely that you could trip Methuselah; and yet if that old person could come back here it is more than likely that one of the first things he would do would be to take hold of one of these electric wires and tie himself all up in a knot. Now the surer thing and the wiser thing would be for him to ask somebody whether it was a good thing to take hold of. But that would not suit him; he would be one of the self-taught kind that go by experience; he would want to examine for himself. And he would find, for his instruction, that the coiled patriarch shuns the electric wire; and it would be useful to him, too, and would leave his education in quite a complete and rounded-out condition, till he should come again, some day, and go to bouncing a dynamite-can around to find out what was in it.

But we wander from the point. However, get a teacher; it saves much time and Pond's Extract.

Before taking final leave of me, my instructor inquired concerning my physical strength, and I was able to inform him that I hadn't any. He said that that was a defect which would make up-hill wheeling pretty difficult for me at first; but he also said the bicycle would soon remove it. The contrast between his muscles and mine was quite marked. He wanted to test mine, so I offered my biceps—which was my best. It almost made him smile. He said, "It is pulpy, and soft, and yielding, and rounded; it evades pressure, and glides from under the fingers; in the dark a body might think it was an oyster in a rag." Perhaps this made me look grieved, for he added, briskly: "Oh, that's all right, you needn't worry about that; in a little while you can't tell it from a petrified kidney. Just go right along with your practice; you're all right."

Then he left me, and I started out alone to seek adventures. You don't really have to seek them—that is nothing but a phrase—they come to you.

I chose a reposeful Sabbath-day sort of a back street which was about thirty yards wide between the curbstones. I knew it was not wide enough; still, I thought that by keeping strict watch and wasting no space unnecessarily I could crowd through.

Of course I had trouble mounting the machine, entirely on my own responsibility, with no encouraging moral support from the outside, no sympathetic instructor to say, "Good! now you're doing well—good again—don't hurry—there, now, you're all right—brace up, go ahead." In place of this I had some other support. This was a boy, who was perched on a gate-post munching a hunk of maple sugar.

He was full of interest and comment. The first time I failed and went down he said that if he was me he would dress up in pillows, that's what he would do. The next time I went down he advised me to go and learn to ride a tricycle first. The third time I collapsed he said he didn't believe I could stay on a horse-car. But the next time I succeeded, and got clumsily under way in a weaving, tottering, uncertain fashion, and occupying pretty much all of the street. My slow and lumbering gait filled the boy to the chin with scorn, and he sung out, "My, but don't he rip along!" Then he got down from his post and loafed along the sidewalk, still observing and occasionally commenting. Presently he dropped into my wake and followed along behind. A little girl passed by, balancing a wash-board on her head, and giggled, and seemed about to make a remark, but the boy said, rebukingly, "Let him alone, he's going to a funeral."

I have been familiar with that street for years, and had always supposed it was a dead level; but it was not, as the bicycle now informed me, to my surprise. The bicycle, in the hands of a novice, is as alert and acute as a spirit-level in the detecting of delicate and vanishing shades of difference in these matters. It notices a rise where your untrained eye would not observe that one existed; it notices any decline which water will run down. I was toiling up a slight rise, but was not aware of it. It made me tug and pant and perspire; and still, labor as I might, the machine came almost to a standstill every little while. At such times the boy would say: "That's it! take a rest—there ain't no hurry. They can't hold the funeral without YOU."

Stones were a bother to me. Even the smallest ones gave me a panic when I went over them. I could hit any kind of a stone, no matter how small, if I tried to miss it; and of course at first I couldn't help trying to do that. It is but natural. It is part of the ass that is put in us all, for some inscrutable reason.

I was at the end of my course, at last, and it was necessary for me to round to. This is not a pleasant thing, when you undertake it for the first time on your own responsibility, and neither is it likely to succeed. Your confidence oozes away, you fill steadily up with nameless apprehensions, every fiber of you is tense with a watchful strain, you start a cautious and gradual curve, but your squirmy nerves are all full of electric anxieties, so the curve is quickly demoralized into a jerky and perilous zigzag; then suddenly the nickel-clad horse takes the bit in its mouth and goes slanting for the curbstone, defying all prayers and all your powers to change its mind—your heart stands still, your breath hangs fire, your legs forget to work, straight on you go, and there are but a couple of feet between you and the curb now. And now is the desperate moment, the last chance to save yourself; of course all your instructions fly out of your head, and you whirl your wheel AWAY from the curb instead of TOWARD it, and so you go sprawling on that granite-bound inhospitable shore.

That was my luck; that was my experience. I dragged myself out from under the indestructible bicycle and sat down on the curb to examine.

I started on the return trip. It was now that I saw a farmer's wagon poking along down toward me, loaded with cabbages. If I needed anything to perfect the precariousness of my steering, it was just that. The farmer was occupying the middle of the road with his wagon, leaving barely fourteen or fifteen yards of space on either side. I couldn't shout at him—a beginner can't shout; if he opens his mouth he is gone; he must keep all his attention on his business. But in this grisly emergency, the boy came to the rescue, and for once I had to be grateful to him. He kept a sharp lookout on the swiftly varying impulses and inspirations of my bicycle, and shouted to the man accordingly:

"To the left! Turn to the left, or this jackass 'll run over you!" The man started to do it. "No, to the right, to the right! Hold on! THAT won't do!—to the left!—to the right!—to the LEFT—right! left—ri—Stay where you ARE, or you're a goner!"

And just then I caught the off horse in the starboard and went down in a pile. I said, "Hang it! Couldn't you SEE I was coming?"

"Yes, I see you was coming, but I couldn't tell which WAY you was coming. Nobody could—now, *could* they? You couldn't yourself—now, *could* you? So what could *I* do?"

There was something in that, and so I had the magnanimity to say so. I said I was no doubt as much to blame as he was.

Within the next five days I achieved so much progress that the boy couldn't keep up with me. He had to go back to his gate-post, and content himself with watching me fall at long range.

There was a row of low stepping-stones across one end of the street, a measured yard apart. Even after I got so I could steer pretty fairly I was so afraid of those stones that I always hit them. They gave me the worst falls I ever got in that street, except those which I got from dogs. I have seen it stated that no expert is quick enough to run over a dog; that a dog is always able to skip out of his way. I think that that may be true: but I think that the reason he couldn't run over the dog was because he was trying to. I did not try to run over any dog. But I ran over every dog that came along. I think it makes a great deal of difference. If you try to run over the dog he knows how to calculate, but if you are trying to miss him he does not know how to calculate, and is liable to jump the wrong way every time. It was always so in my experience. Even when I could not hit a wagon I could hit a dog that came to see me practice. They all liked to see me practice, and they all came, for there was very little going on in our neighborhood to entertain a dog. It took time to learn to miss a dog, but I achieved even that.

I can steer as well as I want to, now, and I will catch that boy out one of these days and run over HIM if he doesn't reform.

Get a bicycle. You will not regret it, if you live.

Written in 1893.
First published in
What Is Man? and Other Essays, 1917.

FENIMORE COOPER'S LITERARY OFFENCES

The Pathfinder and *The Deerslayer* stand at the head of Cooper's novels as artistic creations. There are others of his works which contain parts as perfect as are to be found in these, and scenes even more thrilling. Not one can be compared with either of them as a finished whole. The defects in both of these tales are comparatively slight. They were pure works of art.

—PROF. LOUNSBURY

The five tales reveal an extraordinary fulness of invention. . . . One of the very greatest characters in fiction, Natty Bumppo . . . The craft of the woodsman, the tricks of the trapper, all the delicate art of the forest, were familiar to Cooper from his youth up.

—PROF. BRANDER MATTHEWS

Cooper is the greatest artist in the domain of romantic fiction yet produced by America.

—WILKIE COLLINS

It seems to me that it was far from right for the Professor of English Literature in Yale, the Professor of English Literature in Columbia, and Wilkie Collins to deliver opinions on Cooper's literature without having read some of it. It would have been much more decorous to keep silent and let persons talk who have read Cooper.

Cooper's art has some defects. In one place in 'Deerslayer,' and in the restricted space of two-thirds of a page, Cooper has scored 114 offences against literary art out of a possible 115. It breaks the record.

There are nineteen rules governing literary art in the domain of romantic fiction—some say twenty-two. In Deerslayer Cooper violated eighteen of them.

These eighteen require:

1. That a tale shall accomplish something and arrive somewhere. But the Deerslayer tale accomplishes nothing and arrives in the air.
2. They require that the episodes of a tale shall be necessary parts of the tale, and shall help to develop it. But as the Deerslayer tale is not a tale, and accomplishes nothing and arrives nowhere, the episodes have no rightful place in the work, since there was nothing for them to develop.
3. They require that the personages in a tale shall be alive, except in the case of corpses, and that always the reader shall be able to tell the corpses from the others. But this detail has often been overlooked in the Deerslayer tale.
4. They require that the personages in a tale, both dead and alive, shall exhibit a sufficient excuse for being there. But this detail also has been overlooked in the Deerslayer tale.
5. They require that when the personages of a tale deal in conversation, the talk shall sound like human talk, and be talk such as human beings would be likely to talk in the given circumstances, and have a discoverable meaning, also a discoverable purpose, and a show of relevancy, and remain in the neighborhood of the subject in hand, and be interesting to the reader, and help out the tale, and stop when the people cannot think of anything more to say. But this requirement has been ignored from the beginning of the Deerslayer tale to the end of it.

6. They require that when the author describes the character of a personage in his tale, the conduct and conversation of that personage shall justify said description. But this law gets little or no attention in the Deerslayer tale, as Natty Bumppo's case will amply prove.

7. They require that when a personage talks like an illustrated, gilt-edged, tree-calf, hand-tooled, seven-dollar Friendship's Offering in the beginning of a paragraph, he shall not talk like a negro minstrel in the end of it. But this rule is flung down and danced upon in the Deerslayer tale.

8. They require that crass stupidities shall not be played upon the reader as "the craft of the woodsman, the delicate art of the forest," by either the author or the people in the tale. But this rule is persistently violated in the Deerslayer tale.

9. They require that the personages of a tale shall confine themselves to possibilities and let miracles alone; or, if they venture a miracle, the author must so plausibly set it forth as to make it look possible and reasonable. But these rules are not respected in the Deerslayer tale.

10. They require that the author shall make the reader feel a deep interest in the personages of his tale and in their fate; and that he shall make the reader love the good people in the tale and hate the bad ones. But the reader of the Deerslayer tale dislikes the good people in it, is indifferent to the others, and wishes they would all get drowned together.

11. They require that the characters in a tale shall be so clearly defined that the reader can tell beforehand what each will do in a given emergency. But in the Deerslayer tale this rule is vacated.

In addition to these large rules there are some little ones. These require that the author shall:

12. Say what he is proposing to say, not merely come near it.

13. Use the right word, not its second cousin.

14. Eschew surplusage.

15. Not omit necessary details.

16. Avoid slovenliness of form.
17. Use good grammar.
18. Employ a simple and straightforward style.

Even these seven are coldly and persistently violated in the Deerslayer tale.

Cooper's gift in the way of invention was not a rich endowment; but such as it was he liked to work it, he was pleased with the effects, and indeed he did some quite sweet things with it. In his little box of stage properties he kept six or eight cunning devices, tricks, artifices for his savages and woodsmen to deceive and circumvent each other with, and he was never so happy as when he was working these innocent things and seeing them go. A favorite one was to make a moccasined person tread in the tracks of the moccasined enemy, and thus hide his own trail. Cooper wore out barrels and barrels of moccasins in working that trick. Another stage-property that he pulled out of his box pretty frequently was his broken twig. He prized his broken twig above all the rest of his effects, and worked it the hardest. It is a restful chapter in any book of his when somebody doesn't step on a dry twig and alarm all the reds and whites for two hundred yards around. Every time a Cooper person is in peril, and absolute silence is worth four dollars a minute, he is sure to step on a dry twig. There may be a hundred handier things to step on, but that wouldn't satisfy Cooper. Cooper requires him to turn out and find a dry twig; and if he can't do it, go and borrow one. In fact, the Leather Stocking Series ought to have been called the Broken Twig Series.

I am sorry there is not room to put in a few dozen instances of the delicate art of the forest, as practised by Natty Bumppo and some of the other Cooperian experts. Perhaps we may venture two or three samples. Cooper was a sailor—a naval officer; yet he gravely tells us how a vessel, driving towards a lee shore in a gale, is steered for a particular spot by her skipper because he knows of an undertow there which will hold her back against the gale and save her. For just pure woodcraft, or sailorcraft, or whatever it is, isn't that neat? For several years Cooper was daily in the society of artillery, and he ought to have noticed that when a cannon-ball strikes the ground it either buries itself or skips a hundred feet or so; skips again a hundred feet or so— and so on, till finally it gets tired and rolls. Now in one place he loses some "females"—as he always calls women—in the edge of a wood near a plain at night in a fog, on purpose to give Bumppo a chance to show off the delicate art of the forest before the reader. These mislaid people are hunting for a fort. They hear a cannonblast, and a cannon-ball presently comes rolling into the wood and stops at their feet. To the females this suggests nothing. The case is very different with the admirable Bumppo. I wish I may never know peace again if he doesn't strike out promptly and follow the track of that cannon-ball across the plain through the dense fog and find the fort. Isn't it a daisy? If Cooper had any real knowledge of Nature's ways of doing things, he had a most delicate art in concealing the fact. For instance: one of his acute Indian experts, Chingachgook (pronounced Chicago, I think), has lost the trail of a person he is tracking through the forest. Apparently that trail is hopelessly lost. Neither you nor I could ever have guessed out the way to find it. It was very different with Chicago. Chicago was not stumped for long. He turned a running stream out of its course, and there, in the slush in its old bed, were that person's moccasin-tracks. The current did not wash them away, as it would have done in all other like cases—no, even the eternal laws of Nature have to vacate when Cooper wants to put up a delicate job of woodcraft on the reader.

We must be a little wary when Brander Matthews tells us that Cooper's books "reveal an extraordinary fulness of invention." As a rule, I am quite willing to accept Brander Matthews's literary judgments and applaud his lucid and graceful phrasing of them; but that particular statement needs to be taken with a few tons of salt. Bless your heart, Cooper hadn't any more

THE AMERICAN SATIRIST

invention than a horse; and I don't mean a high-class horse, either; I mean a clothes-horse. It would be very difficult to find a really clever "situation" in Cooper's books, and still more difficult to find one of any kind which he has failed to render absurd by his handling of it. Look at the episodes of "the caves"; and at the celebrated scuffle between Maqua and those others on the table-land a few days later; and at Hurry Harry's queer water-transit from the castle to the ark; and at Deerslayer's half-hour with his first corpse; and at the quarrel between Hurry Harry and Deerslayer later; and at—but choose for yourself; you can't go amiss.

If Cooper had been an observer his inventive faculty would have worked better; not more interestingly, but more rationally, more plausibly. Cooper's proudest creations in the way of "situations" suffer noticeably from the absence of the observer's protecting gift. Cooper's eye was splendidly inaccurate. Cooper seldom saw anything correctly. He saw nearly all things as through a glass eye, darkly. Of course a man who cannot see the commonest little every-day matters accurately is working at a disadvantage when he is constructing a "situation." In the Deerslayer tale Cooper has a stream which is fifty feet wide where it flows out of a lake; it presently narrows to twenty as it meanders along for no given reason; and yet when a stream acts like that it ought to be required to explain itself. Fourteen pages later the width of the brook's outlet from the lake has suddenly shrunk thirty feet, and become "the narrowest part of the stream." This shrinkage is not accounted for. The stream has bends in it, a sure indication that it has alluvial banks and cuts them; yet these bends are only thirty and fifty feet long. If Cooper had been a nice and punctilious observer he would have noticed that the bends were oftener nine hundred feet long than short of it.

Cooper made the exit of that stream fifty feet wide, in the first place, for no particular reason; in the second place, he narrowed it to less than twenty to accommodate some Indians. He bends a "sapling" to the form of an arch over this narrow passage, and conceals six Indians in its foliage. They are "laying" for a settler's scow or ark which is coming up the stream on its way to the lake; it is being hauled against the stiff current by a rope whose stationary end is anchored in the lake; its rate of progress cannot be more than a mile an hour. Cooper describes the ark, but pretty obscurely. In the matter of dimensions "it was little more than a modern canal-boat." Let us guess, then, that it was about one hundred and forty feet long. It was of "greater breadth than common." Let us guess, then, that it was about sixteen feet wide. This leviathan had been prowling down bends which were but a third as long as itself, and scraping between banks where it had only two feet of space to spare on each side. We cannot too much admire this miracle. A low-roofed log dwelling occupies "two-thirds of the ark's length"—a dwelling ninety feet long and sixteen feet wide, let us say a kind of vestibule train. The dwelling has two rooms—each forty-five feet long and sixteen feet wide, let us guess. One of them is the bedroom of the Hutter girls, Judith and Hetty; the other is the parlor in the daytime, at night it is papa's bedchamber. The ark is arriving at the stream's exit now, whose width has been reduced to less than twenty feet to accommodate the Indians—say to eighteen. There is a foot to spare on each side of the boat. Did the Indians notice that there was going to be a tight squeeze there? Did they notice that they could make money by climbing down out of that arched sapling and just stepping aboard when the ark scraped by? No, other Indians would have noticed these things, but Cooper's Indians never notice anything. Cooper thinks they are marvelous creatures for noticing, but he was almost always in error about his Indians. There was seldom a sane one among them.

The ark is one hundred and forty feet long; the dwelling is ninety feet long. The idea of the Indians is to drop softly and secretly from the arched sapling to the dwelling as the ark creeps along under it at the rate of a mile an hour, and butcher the family. It will take the ark a minute and a half to pass under. It will take the ninety foot dwelling a minute to pass under. Now, then, what did the six Indians do? It would take you thirty years to guess, and even then you would have to give it up, I believe. Therefore, I will tell you what the Indians did. Their chief, a person of quite extraordinary intellect for a Cooper Indian, warily watched the canal-boat as it squeezed along under him, and when he had got his calculations fined down to exactly the right shade, as he judged, he let go and dropped. And missed the house! That is actually what he did. He missed the house, and landed in the stern of the scow. It was not much of a fall, yet it knocked him silly. He lay there unconscious. If the house had been ninety-seven feet long he would have made the trip. The fault was Cooper's, not his. The error lay in the construction of the house. Cooper was no architect.

There still remained in the roost five Indians.

The boat has passed under and is now out of their reach. Let me explain what the five did—you would not be able to reason it out for yourself. No. 1 jumped for the boat, but fell in the water astern of it. Then No. 2 jumped for the boat, but fell in the water still farther astern of it. Then No. 3 jumped for the boat, and fell a good way astern of it. Then No. 4 jumped for the boat, and fell in the water away astern. Then even No. 5 made a jump for the boat—for he was a Cooper Indian. In the matter of intellect, the difference between a Cooper Indian and the Indian that stands in front of the cigarshop is not spacious. The scow episode is really a sublime burst of invention; but it does not thrill, because the inaccuracy of the details throws a sort of air of fictitiousness and general improbability over it. This comes of Cooper's inadequacy as an observer.

The reader will find some examples of Cooper's high talent for inaccurate observation in the account of the shooting-match in The Pathfinder.

> *"A common wrought nail was driven lightly into the target, its head having been first touched with paint."*

The color of the paint is not stated—an important omission, but Cooper deals freely in important omissions. No, after all, it was not an important omission; for this nail-head is a hundred yards from the marksmen, and could not be seen by them at that distance, no matter what its color might be.

How far can the best eyes see a common house-fly? A hundred yards? It is quite impossible. Very well; eyes that cannot see a house-fly that is a hundred yards away cannot see an ordinary nailhead at that distance, for the size of the two objects is the same. It takes a keen eye to see a fly or a nailhead at fifty yards— one hundred and fifty feet. Can the reader do it?

The nail was lightly driven, its head painted, and game called. Then the Cooper miracles began. The bullet of the first marksman chipped an edge off the nail-head; the next man's bullet drove the nail a little way into the target—and removed all the paint. Haven't the miracles gone far enough now? Not to suit Cooper; for the purpose of this whole scheme is to show off his prodigy, Deerslayer Hawkeye—Long-Rifle—Leather-Stocking— Pathfinder—Bumppo before the ladies.

> "'Be all ready to clench it, boys!' cried out Pathfinder, stepping into his friend's tracks the instant they were vacant.
>
> 'Never mind a new nail; I can see that, though the paint is gone, and what I can see I can hit at a hundred yards, though it were only a mosquito's eye. Be ready to clench!'
>
> "The rifle cracked, the bullet sped its way, and the head of the nail was buried in the wood, covered by the piece of flattened lead."

There, you see, is a man who could hunt flies with a rifle, and command a ducal salary in a Wild West show to-day if we had him back with us.

The recorded feat is certainly surprising just as it stands; but it is not surprising enough for Cooper. Cooper adds a touch. He has made Pathfinder do this miracle with another man's rifle; and not only that, but Pathfinder did not have even the advantage of loading it himself. He had everything against him, and yet he made that impossible shot; and not only made it, but did it with absolute confidence, saying, "Be ready to clench." Now a person like that would have undertaken that same feat with a brickbat, and with Cooper to help he would have achieved it, too.

Pathfinder showed off handsomely that day before the ladies. His very first feat was a thing which no Wild West show can touch. He was standing with the group of marksmen, observing—a hundred yards from the target, mind; one Jasper raised his rifle and drove the centre of the bull's-eye. Then the Quartermaster fired. The target exhibited no result this time. There was a laugh. "It's a dead miss," said Major Lundie. Pathfinder waited an impressive moment or two; then said, in that calm, indifferent, know-it-all way of his, "No, Major, he has covered Jasper's bullet, as will be seen if any one will take the trouble to examine the target."

Wasn't it remarkable! How could he see that little pellet fly through the air and enter that distant bullet-hole? Yet that is what he did; for nothing is impossible to a Cooper person. Did any of those people have any deep-seated doubts about this thing? No; for that would imply sanity, and these were all Cooper people.

> "The respect for Pathfinder's skill and for his 'quickness
> and accuracy of sight' was so profound and general, that
> the instant he made this declaration the spectators began
> to distrust their own opinions, and a dozen rushed to the
> target in order to ascertain the fact. There, sure enough, it
> was found that the Quartermaster's bullet had gone through
> the hole made by Jasper's, and that, too, so accurately
> as to require a minute examination to be certain of the
> circumstance, which, however, was soon clearly established

by discovering one bullet over the other in the stump against which the target was placed."

They made a "minute" examination; but never mind, how could they know that there were two bullets in that hole without digging the latest one out? for neither probe nor eyesight could prove the presence of any more than one bullet. Did they dig? No; as we shall see. It is the Pathfinder's turn now; he steps out before the ladies, takes aim, and fires.

But, alas! here is a disappointment; an incredible, an unimaginable disappointment—for the target's aspect is unchanged; there is nothing there but that same old bullet-hole!

> *"'If one dared to hint at such a thing,' cried Major Duncan, 'I should say that the Pathfinder has also missed the target!'"*

As nobody had missed it yet, the "also" was not necessary; but never mind about that, for the Pathfinder is going to speak.

> *'No, no, Major,' said he, confidently, 'that would be a risky declaration. I didn't load the piece, and can't say what was in it; but if it was lead, you will find the bullet driving down those of the Quartermaster and Jasper, else is not my name Pathfinder.'*

> *"A shout from the target announced the truth of this assertion."*

Is the miracle sufficient as it stands? Not for Cooper. The Pathfinder speaks again, as he "now slowly advances towards the stage occupied by the females":

> *"That's not all, boys, that's not all; if you find the target touched at all, I'll own to a miss. The Quartermaster cut the wood, but you'll find no wood cut by that last messenger."*

The miracle is at last complete. He knew—doubtless saw—at the distance of a hundred yards—that his bullet had passed into the hole without fraying the edges. There were now three bullets in that one hole—three bullets embedded processionally in the body of the stump back of the target. Everybody knew this—somehow or other—and yet nobody had dug any of them out to make sure. Cooper is not a close observer, but he is interesting. He is certainly always that, no matter what happens. And he is more interesting when he is not noticing what he is about than when he is. This is a considerable merit.

The conversations in the Cooper books have a curious sound in our modern ears. To believe that such talk really ever came out of people's mouths would be to believe that there was a time when time was of no value to a person who thought he had something to say; when it was the custom to spread a two-minute remark out to ten; when a man's mouth was a rolling-mill, and busied itself all day long in turning four-foot pigs of thought into thirty-foot bars of conversational railroad iron by attenuation; when subjects were seldom faithfully stuck to, but the talk wandered all around and arrived nowhere; when conversations consisted mainly of irrelevancies, with here and there a relevancy, a relevancy with an embarrassed look, as not being able to explain how it got there.

Cooper was certainly not a master in the construction of dialogue. Inaccurate observation defeated him here as it defeated him in so many other enterprises of his. He even failed to notice that the man who talks corrupt English six days in the week must and will talk it on the seventh, and can't help himself. In the Deerslayer story he lets Deerslayer talk the showiest kind of book-talk sometimes, and at other times the basest of base dialects. For instance, when some one asks him if he has a sweetheart, and if so, where she abides, this is his majestic answer:

"She's in the forest-hanging from the boughs of the trees, in a soft rain—in the dew on the open grass—the clouds that float about in the blue heavens—the birds that sing in the woods—the sweet springs where I slake my thirst—and in all the other glorious gifts that come from God's Providence!"

And he preceded that, a little before, with this:

"It consarns me as all things that touches a fri'nd consarns a fri'nd."

And this is another of his remarks:

"If I was Injin born, now, I might tell of this, or carry in the scalp and boast of the expl'ite afore the whole tribe; or if my inimy had only been a bear"—and so on.

We cannot imagine such a thing as a veteran Scotch Commander-in-Chief comporting himself in the field like a windy melodramatic actor, but Cooper could. On one occasion Alice and Cora were being chased by the French through a fog in the neighborhood of their father's fort:

"'Point de quartier aux coquins!' cried an eager pursuer, who seemed to direct the operations of the enemy.

"Stand firm and be ready, my gallant 60ths!' suddenly exclaimed a voice above them; wait to see the enemy; fire low, and sweep the glacis.

"'Father? father!' exclaimed a piercing cry from out the mist; 'it is I! Alice! thy own Elsie! spare, O! save your daughters!'

"'Hold!' shouted the former speaker, in the awful tones of parental agony, the sound reaching even to the woods, and

rolling back in solemn echo. "Tis she! God has restored me my children! Throw open the sally-port; to the field, 60ths, to the field! pull not a trigger, lest ye kill my lambs! Drive off these dogs of France with your steel!"'

Cooper's word-sense was singularly dull. When a person has a poor ear for music he will flat and sharp right along without knowing it. He keeps near the tune, but it is not the tune. When a person has a poor ear for words, the result is a literary flatting and sharping; you perceive what he is intending to say, but you also perceive that he doesn't say it. This is Cooper. He was not a word-musician. His ear was satisfied with the approximate word. I will furnish some circumstantial evidence in support of this charge. My instances are gathered from half a dozen pages of the tale called Deerslayer. He uses "verbal," for "oral"; "precision," for "facility"; "phenomena," for "marvels"; "necessary," for "predetermined"; "unsophisticated," for "primitive"; "preparation," for "expectancy"; "rebuked," for "subdued"; "dependent on," for "resulting from"; "fact," for "condition"; "fact," for "conjecture"; "precaution," for "caution"; "explain," for "determine"; "mortified," for "disappointed"; "meretricious," for "factitious"; "materially," for "considerably"; "decreasing," for "deepening"; "increasing," for "disappearing"; "embedded," for "enclosed"; "treacherous;" for "hostile"; "stood," for "stooped"; "softened," for "replaced"; "rejoined," for "remarked"; "situation," for "condition"; "different," for "differing"; "insensible," for "unsentient"; "brevity," for "celerity"; "distrusted," for "suspicious"; "mental imbecility," for "imbecility"; "eyes," for "sight"; "counteracting," for "opposing"; "funeral obsequies," for "obsequies."

There have been daring people in the world who claimed that Cooper could write English, but they are all dead now—all dead but Lounsbury. I don't remember that Lounsbury makes the claim in so many words, still he makes it, for he says that Deerslayer is a "pure work of art." Pure, in that connection, means faultless—faultless in all details—and language is a detail. If Mr. Lounsbury had only compared Cooper's English with the English which he writes himself—but it is plain that he didn't; and so it is likely that he imagines until this day that Cooper's is as clean and compact as his own. Now I feel sure, deep down in my heart, that Cooper wrote about the poorest English that exists in our language, and that the English of Deerslayer is the very worst that even Cooper ever wrote.

I may be mistaken, but it does seem to me that Deerslayer is not a work of art in any sense; it does seem to me that it is destitute of every detail that goes to the making of a work of art; in truth, it seems to me that Deerslayer is just simply a literary delirium tremens.

A work of art? It has no invention; it has no order, system, sequence, or result; it has no lifelikeness, no thrill, no stir, no seeming of reality; its characters are confusedly drawn, and by their acts and words they prove that they are not the sort of people the author claims that they are; its humor is pathetic; its pathos is funny; its conversations are—oh! indescribable; its love-scenes odious; its English a crime against the language.

Counting these out, what is left is Art. I think we must all admit that.

First published in 1895.

A
PRESIDENTIAL CANDIDATE

———————————

I have pretty much made up my mind to run for President. What the country wants is a candidate who cannot be injured by investigation of his past history, so that the enemies of the party will be unable to rake up anything against him that nobody ever heard of before. If you know the worst about a candidate, to begin with, every attempt to spring things on him will be checkmated. Now I am going to enter the field with an open record. I am going to own up in advance to all the wickedness I have done, and if any Congressional committee is disposed to prowl around my biography in the hope of discovering any dark and deadly deed that I have secreted, why—let it prowl. In the first place, I admit that I treed a rheumatic grandfather of mine in the winter of 1850. He was old and inexpert in climbing trees, but with the heartless brutality that is characteristic of me I ran him out of the front door in his night- shirt at the point of a shotgun, and caused him to bowl up a maple tree, where he remained all night, while I emptied shot into his legs. I did this because he snored. I will do it again if I ever have another grandfather. I am as inhuman now as I was in 1850. I candidly acknowledge that I ran away at the battle of Gettysburg. My friends have tried to smooth over this fact by asserting that I did so for the purpose of imitating Washington, who went into the woods at Valley Forge for the purpose of saying his prayers. It was a miserable subterfuge. I struck out in a straight line for the Tropic of Cancer because I was scared. I wanted my country saved, but I preferred to have somebody else save it. I entertain that preference yet. If the bubble reputation can be obtained only at the cannon's mouth, I am willing to go there for it, provided the cannon is empty. If it is loaded my immortal and inflexible purpose is to get over the fence and go home. My invariable practice in war has been to bring out of every fight two-thirds more men than when I went in. This seems to me to be Napoleonic in its grandeur. My financial views are of the most decided character, but they are not likely, perhaps, to increase my popularity with the advocates of inflation. I do not insist upon the special supremacy of rag money or hard money. The great fundamental principle of my life is to take any kind I can get. The rumor that I buried a dead aunt under my grapevine was correct. The vine needed fertilizing, my aunt had to be buried, and I dedicated her to this high purpose. Does that unfit me for the Presidency? The Constitution of our country does not say so. No other citizen was ever considered unworthy of this office because he enriched his grapevines with his dead relatives. Why should I be selected as the first victim of an absurd prejudice? I admit also that I am not a friend of the poor man. I regard the poor man, in his present condition, as so much wasted raw material. Cut up and properly canned, he might be made useful to fatten the natives of the cannibal islands and to improve our export trade with that region. I shall recommend legislation upon the subject in my first message. My campaign cry will be: "Desiccate the poor workingman; stuff him into sausages." These are about the worst parts of my record. On them I come before the country. If my country don't want me, I will go back again. But I recommend myself as a safe man—a man who starts from the basis of total depravity and proposes to be fiendish to the last.

First published in 1879.

ADVICE TO
LITTLE GIRLS

Good little girls ought not to make mouths at their teachers for every trifling offense. This retaliation should only be resorted to under peculiarly aggravated circumstances.

If you have nothing but a rag-doll stuffed with sawdust, while one of your more fortunate little playmates has a costly China one, you should treat her with a show of kindness nevertheless. And you ought not to attempt to make a forcible swap with her unless your conscience would justify you in it, and you know you are able to do it.

You ought never to take your little brother's "chewing-gum" away from him by main force; it is better to rope him in with the promise of the first two dollars and a half you find floating down the river on a grindstone. In the artless simplicity natural to this time of life, he will regard it as a perfectly fair transaction. In all ages of the world this eminently plausible fiction has lured the obtuse infant to financial ruin and disaster.

If at any time you find it necessary to correct your brother, do not correct him with mud—never, on any account, throw mud at him, because it will spoil his clothes. It is better to scald him a little, for then you obtain desirable results. You secure his immediate attention to the lessons you are inculcating, and at the same time your hot water will have a tendency to move impurities from his person, and possibly the skin, in spots.

If your mother tells you to do a thing, it is wrong to reply that you won't. It is better and more becoming to intimate that you will do as she bids you, and then afterward act quietly in the matter according to the dictates of your best judgment.

You should ever bear in mind that it is to your kind parents that you are indebted for your food, and for the privilege of staying home from school when you let on that you are sick. Therefore you ought to respect their little prejudices, and humor their little whims, and put up with their little foibles until they get to crowding you too much.

Good little girls always show marked deference for the aged. You ought never to "sass" old people unless they "sass" you first.

First published in 1867.

PRIVATE HISTORY OF THE "JUMPING FROG" STORY

FIVE or six years ago a lady from Finland asked me to tell her a story in our negro dialect, so that she could get an idea of what that variety of speech was like. I told her one of Hopkinson Smith's negro stories, and gave her a copy of *Harper's Monthly* containing it. She translated it for a Swedish newspaper, but by an oversight named me as the author of it instead of Smith. I was very sorry for that, because I got a good lashing in the Swedish press, which would have fallen to his share but for that mistake; for it was shown that Boccaccio had told that very story, in his curt and meager fashion, five hundred years before Smith took hold of it and made a good and tellable thing out of it.

I have always been sorry for Smith. But my own turn has come now. A few weeks ago Professor Van Dyke, of Princeton, asked this question:

"Do you know how old your Jumping Frog story is?"

And I answered:

"Yes—forty-five years. The thing happened in Calaveras County in the spring of 1849."

"No; it happened earlier—a couple of thousand years earlier; it is a Greek story."

I was astonished and hurt. I said:

"I am willing to be a literary thief if it has been so ordained; I am even willing to be caught robbing the ancient dead alongside of Hopkinson Smith, for he is my friend and a good fellow, and I think would be as honest as any one if he could do it without occasioning remark; but I am not willing to ante date his crimes by fifteen hundred years. I must ask you to knock off part of that."

But the professor was not chaffing; he was in earnest, and could not abate a century. He named the Greek author, and offered to get the book and send it to me and the college text-book containing the English translation also. I thought I would like the translation best, because Greek makes me tired. January 30th he sent me the English version, and I will presently insert it in this article. It is my Jumping Frog tale in every essential. It is not strung out as I have strung it out, but it is all there.

To me this is very curious and interesting. Curious for several reasons. For instance:

I heard the story told by a man who was not telling it to his hearers as a thing new to them, but as a thing which *they had witnessed and would remember.* He was a dull person, and ignorant; he had no gift as a story-teller, and no invention; in his mouth this episode was merely history—history and statistics; and the gravest sort of history, too; he was entirely serious, for he was dealing with what to him were austere facts, and they interested him solely because they *were* facts; he was drawing on his memory, not his mind; he saw no humor in his tale, neither did his listeners; neither he nor they ever smiled or laughed; in my time I have not attended a more solemn conference. To him and to his fellow gold-miners there were just two things in the story that were worth considering. One was the smartness of the stranger in taking in its hero, Jim Smiley, with a loaded frog; and the other was the stranger's deep knowledge of a frog's nature—for he knew (as the narrator asserted and the listeners conceded) that a frog *likes shot* and is always ready to eat it. Those men discussed those two points, and those only. They were hearty in their admiration of them, and none of the party was aware that a first-rate story had been told in a first-rate way, and that it was brimful of a quality whose presence they never suspected—humor.

Now, then, the interesting question is, *did* the frog episode happen in Angel's Camp in the spring of 49, as told in my hearing that day in the fall of 1865? I am perfectly sure that it did. I am also sure that its duplicate happened in Bœotia a couple of thousand years ago. I think it must be a case of history actually repeating itself, and not a case of a good story floating down the ages and surviving be cause too good to be allowed to perish.

I would now like to have the reader examine the Greek story and the story told by the dull and solemn Californian, and observe how exactly alike they are in essentials.

TRANSLATION

THE ATHENIAN AND THE FROG

An Athenian once fell in with a Bœotian who was sitting by the roadside looking at a frog. Seeing the other approach, the Bœotian said his was a remarkable frog, and asked if he would agree to start a contest of frogs, on condition that he whose frog jumped farthest should receive a large sum of money. The Athenian replied that he would if the other would fetch him a frog, for the lake was near. To this he agreed, and when he was gone the Athenian took the frog, and, opening its mouth, poured some stones into its stomach, so that it did not indeed seem larger than before, but could not jump. The Bœotian soon returned with the other frog, and the contest began. The second frog first was pinched, and jumped moderately; then they pinched the Bœotian frog. And he gathered himself for a leap, and used the utmost effort, but he could not move his body the least. So the Athenian departed with the money. When he was gone the Bœotian, wondering what was the matter with the frog, lifted him up and examined him. And being turned upside down, he opened his mouth and vomited out the stones.

* * * * *

71

And here is the way it happened in California:

FROM
"THE CELEBRATED JUMPING
FROG OF CALAVERAS COUNTY"

Well, thish-yer Smiley had rat-tarriers, and chicken cocks, and tom-cats, and all them kind of things, till you couldn't rest, and you couldn't fetch nothing for him to bet on but he'd match you. He ketched a frog one day, and took him home, and said he cal'lated to educate him; and so he never done nothing for three months but set in his back yard and learn that frog to jump. And you bet you he *did* learn him, too. He'd give him a little punch behind, and the next minute you'd see that frog whirling in the air like a doughnut—see him turn one summerset, or maybe a couple if he got a good start, and come down flat-footed and all right, like a cat. He got him up so in the matter of ketching flies, and kep him in practice so constant, that he'd nail a fly every time as fur as he could see him. Smiley said all a frog wanted was education, and he could do 'most anything—and I believe him. Why, I've seen him set Dan'l Webster down here on this floor—Dan'l Webster was the name of the frog—and sing out "Flies, Dan'l, flies!" and quicker'n you could wink he'd spring straight up and snake a fly off'n the counter there, and flop down on the floor ag'in as solid as a gob of mud, and fall to scratching the side of his head with his hind foot as indifferent as if he hadn't no idea he'd been doin any more'n any frog might do. You never see a frog so modest and straightforward as he was, for all he was so gifted. And when it come to fair and square jumping on a dead level, he could get over more ground at one straddle than any animal of his breed you ever see. Jumping on a dead level was his strong suit, you understand; and when it came to that, Smiley would ante up money on him as long as he had a red. Smiley was monstrous proud of his frog, and well he might be, for fellers that had traveled and been everywheres all said he laid over any frog that ever *they* see.

Well, Smiley kep' the beast in a little lattice box, and he used to fetch him down-town sometimes and lay for a bet. One day a feller—a stranger in the camp, he was—come acrost him with his box, and says:

"What might it be that you've got in the box?""

And Smiley says, sorter indifferent-like, "It might be a parrot, or it might be a canary, maybe, but it ain't—it's only just a frog."

And the feller took it, and looked at it careful, and turned it round this way and that, and says, "H'm—so 'tis. Well, what's *he* good for?"

"Well," Smiley says, easy and careless, "he's good enough for *one* thing, I should judge—he can out jump any frog in Calaveras County."

The feller took the box again and took another long, particular look, and gave it back to Smiley, and says, very deliberate, "Well," he says, "I don't see no p'ints about that frog that's any better'n any other frog."

"Maybe you don't," Smiley says. "Maybe you understand frogs and maybe you don t understand em; maybe you've had experience, and maybe you ain't only a amature, as it were. Anyways, I've got *my* opinion, and I'll resk forty dollars that he can out jump any frog in Calaveras County."

And the feller studies a minute, and then says, kinder sad-like, "Well, I'm only a stranger here, and I ain t got no frog, but if I had a frog I d bet you."

And then Smiley says: "That s all right—that's all right—if you'll hold my box a minute, I'll go and get you a frog." And so the feller took the box and put up his forty dollars along with Smiley's and set down to wait.

So he set there a good while thinking and thinking to hisself, and then he got the frog out and prized his mouth open and took a teaspoon and filled him full of quail-shot—filled him pretty near up to his chin—and set him on the floor. Smiley he went to the swamp and slopped around in the mud for a long time, and finally he ketched a frog and fetched him in and give him to this feller, and says:

"Now, if you're ready, set him alongside of Dan'l, with his fore paws just even with Dan'l's, and I'll give the word." Then he says, "One—two—three—*git!*" and him and the feller touched up the frogs from behind, and the new frog hopped off lively; but Dan'l give a heave, and hysted up his shoulders—so like a Frenchman, but it warn't no use—he couldn't budge; he was planted as solid as a church, and he couldn't no more stir than if he was anchored out. Smiley was a good deal surprised, and he was disgusted, too, but he didn't have no idea what the matter was, of course.

The feller took the money and started away; and when he was going out at the door he sorter jerked his thumb over his shoulder—so—at Dan'l, and says again, very deliberate: "Well," he says, "*I* don't see no p'ints about that frog that's any better'n any other frog."

Smiley he stood scratching his head and looking down at Dan'l a long time, and at last he says, "I do wonder what in the nation that frog throw'd off for—I wonder if there ain't some thing the matter with him—he 'pears to look mighty baggy, somehow." And he ketched Dan'l by the nap of the neck, and hefted him, and says, "Why, blame my cats if he don't weigh five pound!" and turned him upside down, and he belched out a double handful of shot. And then he see how it was, and he was the maddest man—he set the frog down and took out after that feller, but he never ketched him.

* * * * *

The resemblances are deliciously exact. There you have the wily Bœotian and the wily Jim Smiley waiting—two thousand years apart—and waiting, each equipped with his frog and "laying" for the stranger. A contest is proposed—for money. The Athenian would take a chance "if the other would fetch him

a frog"; the Yankee says: "I'm only a stranger here, and I ain t
got no frog; but if I had a frog I'd bet you." The wily Bœotian
and the wily Californian, with that vast gulf of two thousand
years between, retire eagerly and go frogging in the marsh;
the Athenian and the Yankee remain behind and work a base
advantage, the one with pebbles, the other with shot. Presently
the contest began. In the one case "they pinched the Bœotian
frog"; in the other, "him and the feller touched up the frogs
from behind." The Boeotian frog "gathered himself for a leap"
(you can just *see* him!), "but could not move his body in the
least"; the Californian frog "give a heave, but it warn't no use
he couldn t budge." In both the ancient and the modern cases
the strangers departed with the money. The Boeotian and the
Californian wonder what is the matter with their frogs; they lift
them and examine; they turn them upside down and out spills
the informing ballast.

Yes, the resemblances are curiously exact. I used to tell the
story of the Jumping Frog in San Francisco, and presently
Artemus Ward came along and wanted it to help fill out a little
book which he was about to publish; so I wrote it out and sent
it to his publisher, Carleton; but Carleton thought the book had
enough matter in it, so he gave the story to Henry Clapp as a
present, and Clapp put it in his *Saturday Press*, and it killed that
paper with a suddenness that was beyond praise. At least the
paper died with that issue, and none but envious people have
ever tried to rob me of the honor and credit of killing it. The
"Jumping Frog" was the first piece of writing of mine that spread
itself through the newspapers and brought me into public notice.
Consequently, the *Saturday Press* was a cocoon and I the worm
in it; also, I was the gay-colored literary moth which its death set
free. This simile has been used before.

Early in 66 the "Jumping Frog" was issued in book form,
with other sketches of mine. A year or two later Madame Blanc
translated it into French and published it in the *Revue des Deux
Mondes*, but the result was not what should have been expected,

for the *Revue* struggled along and pulled through, and is alive yet. I think the fault must have been in the translation. I ought to have translated it myself. I think so because I examined into the matter and finally retranslated the sketch from the French back into English, to see what the trouble was; that is, to see just what sort of a focus the French people got upon it. Then the mystery was explained. In French the story is too confused, and chaotic, and unreposeful, and ungrammatical, and insane; consequently it could only cause grief and sickness—it could not kill. A glance at my retranslation will show the reader that this must be true.

MY RETRANSLATION

THE FROG JUMPING OF
THE COUNTY OF CALAVERAS

Eh bien! this Smiley nourished some terriers à rats, and some cocks of combat, and some cats, and all sort of things; and with his rage of betting one no had more of repose. He trapped one day a frog and him imported with him (*et l'emporta chez lui*) saying that he pretended to make his education. You me believe if you will, but during three months he not has nothing done but to him apprehend to jump (*apprendre à sauter*) in a court retired of her mansion (*de sa maison*). And I you respond that he have succeeded. He him gives a small blow by behind, and the instant after you shall see the frog turn in the air like a grease-biscuit, make one summersault, sometimes two, when she was well started, and re-fall upon his feet like a cat. He him had accomplished in the art of to gobble the flies (*gober des mouches*), and him there exercised continually—so well that a fly at the most far that she appeared was a fly lost. Smiley had custom to say that all which lacked to a frog it was the education, but with the education she could do nearly all—and I him believe. *Tenez,* I him have seen pose Daniel Webster there upon this plank—

Daniel Webster was the name of the frog—and to him sing, "Some flies, Daniel, some flies!"—in a flash of the eye Daniel had bounded and seized a fly here upon the counter, then jumped anew at the earth, where he rested truly to himself scratch the head with his behind-foot, as if he no had not the least idea of his superiority. Never you not have seen frog as modest, as natural, sweet as she was. And when he himself agitated to jump purely and simply upon plain earth, she does more ground in one jump than any beast of his species than you can know.

To jump plain—this was his strong. When he himself agitated for that Smiley multiplied the bets upon her as long as there to him remained a red. It must to know, Smiley was monstrously proud of his frog, and he of it was right, for some men who were traveled, who had all seen, said that they to him would be injurious to him compare to another frog. Smiley guarded Daniel in a little box latticed which he carried by times to the village for some bet.

One day an individual stranger at the camp him arrested with his box and him said:

"What is this that you have then shut up there within?"

Smiley said, with an air indifferent:

"That could be a paroquet, or a syringe (*ou un serin*), but this no is nothing of such, it not is but a frog."

The individual it took, it regarded with care, it turned from one side and from the other, then he said:

"*Tiens!* in effect!—At what is she good?"

"My God!" respond Smiley, always with an air disengaged, "she is good for one thing, to my notice (*à mon avis*), she can batter in jumping (*elle pent batter en sautant*) all frogs of the county of Calaveras."

The individual re-took the box, it examined of new longly, and it rendered to Smiley in saying with an air deliberate:

"*Eh bien!* I no saw not that that frog had nothing of better than each frog." (*Je ne vois pas que cette grenouille ait rien de mieux qi'aucune grenouille.*) [If that isn't grammar gone to seed, then I count myself no judge. M. T.]

"Possible that you not it saw not," said Smiley, "possible that you you comprehend frogs; possible that you not you there comprehend nothing; possible that you had of the experience, and possible that you not be but an amateur. Of all manner (*De toute manière*) I bet forty dollars that she batter in jumping no matter which frog of the county of Calaveras."

The individual reflected a second, and said like sad:

"I not am but a stranger here, I no have not a frog; but if I of it had one, I would embrace the bet."

"Strong, well!" respond Smiley; "nothing of more facility. If you will hold my box a minute, I go you to search a frog (*j'irai vous chercher*)."

Behold, then, the individual, who guards the box, who puts his forty dollars upon those of Smiley, and who attends (*et qui attend*). He attended enough longtimes, reflecting all solely. And figure you that he takes Daniel, him opens the mouth by force and with a teaspoon him fills with shot of the hunt, even him fills just to the chin, then he him puts by the earth. Smiley during these times was at slopping in a swamp. Finally he trapped (*attrape*) a frog, him carried to that individual, and said:

"Now if you be ready, put him all against Daniel, with their before-feet upon the same line, and I give the signal"—then he added: "One, two, three—advance!"

Him and the individual touched their frogs by behind, and the frog new put to jump smartly, but Daniel himself lifted ponderously, exalted the shoulders thus, like a Frenchman—to what good? he could not budge, he is planted solid like a church, he not advance no more than if one him had put at the anchor.

Smiley was surprised and disgusted, but he not himself doubted not of the turn being intended (*mais i! ne se doutait pas du tour bien entendu*). The individual empocketed the silver, himself with it went, and of it himself in going is that he no gives not a jerk of thumb over the shoulder—like that—at the poor Daniel, in saying with his air deliberate—(*L'individu empoche l'argent s'en va et en s'en allant est ce qu'il ne donne pas un coup de pouce par-dessus l'épaule, comme ça, au pauvre Daniel, en disant de son air delibere.)*

"Eh bein! I no see not that that frog has nothing of better than another."

Smiley himself scratched longtimes the head, the eyes fixed upon Daniel, until that which at last he said:

"I me demand how the devil it makes itself that this beast has refused. Is it that she had something? One would believe that she is stuffed."

He grasped Daniel by the skin of the neck, him lifted and said: "The wolf me bite if he no weigh not five pounds."

He him reversed and the unhappy belched two handfuls of shot (*et le malheureux,* etc.). When Smiley recognized how it was, he was like mad. He deposited his frog by the earth and ran after the individual, but he not him caught never.

* * * * *

It may be that there are people who can translate better than I can, but I am not acquainted with them.

So ends the private and public history of the Jumping Frog of Calaveras County, an incident which has this unique feature about it that it is both old and new, a "chestnut" and not a "chestnut"; for it was original when it happened two thousand years ago, and was again original when it happened in California in our own time.

First published in 1865.

BOOKS AND BURGLARS

Address to the
Redding (Conn.) Library Association,
October 28, 1908

Suppose this library had been in operation a few weeks ago, and the burglars who happened along and broke into my house—taking a lot of things they didn't need, and for that matter which I didn't need—had first made entry into this institution.

Picture them seated here on the floor, poring by the light of their dark-lanterns over some of the books they found, and thus absorbing moral truths and getting a moral uplift. The whole course of their lives would have been changed. As it was, they kept straight on in their immoral way and were sent to jail.

For all we know, they may next be sent to Congress.

And, speaking of burglars, let us not speak of them too harshly. Now, I have known so many burglars—not exactly known, but so many of them have come near me in my various dwelling-places, that I am disposed to allow them credit for whatever good qualities they possess.

Chief among these, and, indeed, the only one I just now think of, is their great care while doing business to avoid disturbing people's sleep.

Noiseless as they may be while at work, however, the effect of their visitation is to murder sleep later on.

Now we are prepared for these visitors. All sorts of alarm devices have been put in the house, and the ground for half a mile around it has been electrified. The burglar who steps within this danger zone will set loose a bedlam of sounds, and spring into readiness for action our elaborate system of defences. As for the fate of the trespasser, do not seek to know that. He will never be heard of more.

"MARK TWAIN'S
FIRST APPEARANCE"

On October 5, 1906, Mr. Clemens, following a musical
recital by his daughter in Norfolk, Conn., addressed
her audience on the subject of stage-fright. He thanked
the people for making things as easy as possible for his
daughter's American debut as a contralto, and then told of
his first experience before the public.

My heart goes out in sympathy to any one who is making his
first appearance before an audience of human beings. By a direct
process of memory I go back forty years, less one month—for
I'm older than I look.

I recall the occasion of my first appearance. San Francisco
knew me then only as a reporter, and I was to make my bow
to San Francisco as a lecturer. I knew that nothing short of
compulsion would get me to the theatre. So I bound myself by
a hard-and-fast contract so that I could not escape. I got to the
theatre forty-five minutes before the hour set for the lecture. My
knees were shaking so that I didn't know whether I could stand
up. If there is an awful, horrible malady in the world, it is stage-
fright-and seasickness. They are a pair. I had stage-fright then
for the first and last time. I was only seasick once, too. It was on
a little ship on which there were two hundred other passengers.
I—was—sick. I was so sick that there wasn't any left for those
other two hundred passengers.

It was dark and lonely behind the scenes in that theatre, and I
peeked through the little peekholes they have in theatre curtains

and looked into the big auditorium. That was dark and empty, too. By-and-by it lighted up, and the audience began to arrive.

I had got a number of friends of mine, stalwart men, to sprinkle themselves through the audience armed with big clubs. Every time I said anything they could possibly guess I intended to be funny they were to pound those clubs on the floor. Then there was a kind lady in a box up there, also a good friend of mine, the wife of the Governor. She was to watch me intently, and whenever I glanced toward her she was going to deliver a gubernatorial laugh that would lead the whole audience into applause.

At last I began. I had the manuscript tucked under a United States flag in front of me where I could get at it in case of need. But I managed to get started without it. I walked up and down—I was young in those days and needed the exercise—and talked and talked.

Right in the middle of the speech I had placed a gem. I had put in a moving, pathetic part which was to get at the hearts and souls of my hearers. When I delivered it they did just what I hoped and expected. They sat silent and awed. I had touched them. Then I happened to glance up at the box where the Governor's wife was—you know what happened.

Well, after the first agonizing five minutes, my stage-fright left me, never to return. I know if I was going to be hanged I could get up and make a good showing, and I intend to. But I shall never forget my feelings before the agony left me, and I got up here to thank you for her for helping my daughter, by your kindness, to live through her first appearance. And I want to thank you for your appreciation of her singing, which is, by-the-way, hereditary.

MORALS AND MEMORY

Mr. Clemens was the guest of honor at a reception held at
Barnard College (Columbia University), March 7, 1906, by
the Barnard Union. One of the young ladies presented Mr.
Clemens, and thanked him for his amiability in coming to
make them an address. She closed with the expression of
the great joy it gave her fellow-collegians, "because we all
love you."

If any one here loves me, she has my sincere thanks. Nay, if
any one here is so good as to love me—why, I'll be a brother to
her. She shall have my sincere, warm, unsullied affection. When
I was coming up in the car with the very kind young lady who
was delegated to show me the way, she asked me what I was
going to talk about. And I said I wasn't sure. I said I had some
illustrations, and I was going to bring them in. I said I was
certain to give those illustrations, but that I hadn't the faintest
notion what they were going to illustrate.

Now, I've been thinking it over in this forest glade [indicating
the woods of Arcady on the scene setting], and I've decided to
work them in with something about morals and the caprices of
memory. That seems to me to be a pretty good subject. You see,
everybody has a memory and it's pretty sure to have caprices.
And, of course, everybody has morals.

It's my opinion that every one I know has morals, though I
wouldn't like to ask. I know I have. But I'd rather teach them
than practice them any day. "Give them to others"—that's my
motto. Then you never have any use for them when you're left

85

without. Now, speaking of the caprices of memory in general, and of mine in particular, it's strange to think of all the tricks this little mental process plays on us. Here we're endowed with a faculty of mind that ought to be more supremely serviceable to us than them all. And what happens? This memory of ours stores up a perfect record of the most useless facts and anecdotes and experiences. And all the things that we ought to know—that we need to know—that we'd profit by knowing—it casts aside with the careless indifference of a girl refusing her true lover. It's terrible to think of this phenomenon. I tremble in all my members when I consider all the really valuable things that I've forgotten in seventy years—when I meditate upon the caprices of my memory.

There's a bird out in California that is one perfect symbol of the human memory. I've forgotten the bird's name (just because it would be valuable for me to know it—to recall it to your own minds, perhaps).

But this fool of a creature goes around collecting the most ridiculous things you can imagine and storing them up. He never selects a thing that could ever prove of the slightest help to him; but he goes about gathering iron forks, and spoons, and tin cans, and broken mouse-traps—all sorts of rubbish that is difficult for him to carry and yet be any use when he gets it. Why, that bird will go by a gold watch to bring back one of those patent cake-pans.

Now, my mind is just like that, and my mind isn't very different from yours—and so our minds are just like that bird. We pass by what would be of inestimable value to us, and pack our memories with the most trivial odds and ends that never by any chance, under any circumstances whatsoever, could be of the slightest use to any one.

Now, things that I have remembered are constantly popping into my head. And I am repeatedly startled by the vividness with which they recur to me after the lapse of years and their utter uselessness in being remembered at all.

I was thinking over some on my way up here. They were the illustrations I spoke about to the young lady on the way up. And I've come to the conclusion, curious though it is, that I can use every one of these freaks of memory to teach you all a lesson. I'm convinced that each one has its moral. And I think it's my duty to hand the moral on to you.

Now, I recall that when I was a boy I was a good boy—I was a very good boy. Why, I was the best boy in my school. I was the best boy in that little Mississippi town where I lived. The population was only about twenty million. You may not believe it, but I was the best boy in that State—and in the United States, for that matter.

But I don't know why I never heard any one say that but myself. I always recognized it. But even those nearest and dearest to me couldn't seem to see it. My mother, especially, seemed to think there was something wrong with that estimate. And she never got over that prejudice.

Now, when my mother got to be eighty-five years old her memory failed her. She forgot little threads that hold life's patches of meaning together. She was living out West then, and I went on to visit her.

I hadn't seen my mother in a year or so. And when I got there she knew my face; knew I was married; knew I had a family, and that I was living with them. But she couldn't, for the life of her, tell my name or who I was. So I told her I was her boy.

"But you don't live with me," she said.

"No," said I, "I'm living in Rochester."

"What are you doing there?"

"Going to school."

"Large school?"

"Very large."

"All boys?"

"All boys."

"And how do you stand?" said my mother.

"I'm the best boy in that school," I answered.

"Well," said my mother, with a return of her old fire, "I'd like to know what the other boys are like."

Now, one point in this story is the fact that my mother's mind went back to my school days, and remembered my little youthful self-prejudice when she'd forgotten everything else about me.

The other point is the moral. There's one there that you will find if you search for it.

Now, here's something else I remember. It's about the first time I ever stole a watermelon. "Stole" is a strong word. Stole? Stole? No, I don't mean that. It was the first time I ever withdrew a watermelon. It was the first time I ever extracted a watermelon. That is exactly the word I want—"extracted." It is definite. It is precise. It perfectly conveys my idea. Its use in dentistry connotes the delicate shade of meaning I am looking for. You know we never extract our own teeth.

And it was not my watermelon that I extracted. I extracted that watermelon from a farmer's wagon while he was inside negotiating with another customer. I carried that watermelon to one of the secluded recesses of the lumber-yard, and there I broke it open.

It was a green watermelon.

Well, do you know when I saw that I began to feel sorry— sorry—sorry. It seemed to me that I had done wrong. I reflected deeply. I reflected that I was young—I think I was just eleven. But I knew that though immature I did not lack moral advancement. I knew what a boy ought to do who had extracted a watermelon—like that.

I considered George Washington, and what action he would have taken under similar circumstances. Then I knew there was just one thing to make me feel right inside, and that was— Restitution.

So I said to myself: "I will do that. I will take that green watermelon back where I got it from." And the minute I had said it I felt that great moral uplift that comes to you when you've made a noble resolution.

So I gathered up the biggest fragments, and I carried them back to the farmer's wagon, and I restored the watermelon— what was left of it. And I made him give me a good one in place of it, too.

And I told him he ought to be ashamed of himself going around working off his worthless, old, green watermelons on trusting purchasers who had to rely on him. How could they tell from the outside whether the melons were good or not? That was his business. And if he didn't reform, I told him I'd see that he didn't get any more of my trade—nor anybody else's I knew, if I could help it.

You know that man was as contrite as a revivalist's last convert. He said he was all broken up to think I'd gotten a green watermelon. He promised that he would never carry another green watermelon if he starved for it. And he drove off—a better man.

Now, do you see what I did for that man? He was on a downward path, and I rescued him. But all I got out of it was a watermelon.

Yet I'd rather have that memory—just that memory of the good I did for that depraved farmer—than all the material gain you can think of. Look at the lesson he got! I never got anything like that from it. But I ought to be satisfied: I was only eleven years old, but I secured everlasting benefit to other people.

The moral in this is perfectly clear, and I think there's one in the next memory I'm going to tell you about.

To go back to my childhood, there's another little incident that comes to me from which you can draw even another moral. It's about one of the times I went fishing. You see, in our house there was a sort of family prejudice against going fishing if you hadn't permission. But it would frequently be bad judgment to ask. So I went fishing secretly, as it were—way up the Mississippi. It was an exquisitely happy trip, I recall, with a very pleasant sensation.

Well, while I was away there was a tragedy in our town. A stranger, stopping over on his way East from California; was

---

stabbed to death in an unseemly brawl.

Now, my father was justice of the peace, and because he was justice of the peace he was coroner; and since he was coroner he was also constable; and being constable he was sheriff; and out of consideration for his holding the office of sheriff he was likewise county clerk and a dozen other officials I don't think of just this minute.

I thought he had power of life or death, only he didn't use it over other boys. He was sort of an austere man. Somehow I didn't like being round him when I'd done anything he disapproved of. So that's the reason I wasn't often around.

Well, when this gentleman got knifed they communicated with the proper authority, the coroner, and they laid the corpse out in the coroner's office—our front sitting-room—in preparation for the inquest the next morning.

About 9 or 10 o'clock I got back from fishing. It was a little too late for me to be received by my folks, so I took my shoes off and slipped noiselessly up the back way to the sitting-room. I was very tired, and I didn't wish to disturb my people. So I groped my way to the sofa and lay down.

Now, I didn't know anything of what had happened during my absence. But I was sort of nervous on my own account-afraid of being caught, and rather dubious about the morning affair. And I had been lying there a few moments when my eyes gradually got used to the darkness, and I became aware of something on the other side of the room.

It was something foreign to the apartment. It had an uncanny appearance. And I sat up looking very hard, and wondering what in heaven this long, formless, vicious-looking thing might be.

First I thought I'd go and see. Then I thought, "Never mind that."

Mind you, I had no cowardly sensations whatever, but it didn't seem exactly prudent to investigate. But I somehow couldn't keep my eyes off the thing. And the more I looked at it the more disagreeably it grew on me. But I was resolved to play the man.

So I decided to turn over and count a hundred, and let the patch of moonlight creep up and show me what the dickens it was.

I turned over and tried to count, but I couldn't keep my mind on it. I kept thinking of that grewsome mass. I was losing count all the time, and going back and beginning over again. Oh no; I wasn't frightened—just annoyed. But by the time I'd gotten to the century mark I turned cautiously over and opened my eyes with great fortitude.

The moonlight revealed to me a marble-white human hand. Well, maybe I wasn't embarrassed! But then that changed to a creepy feeling again, and I thought I'd try the counting again. I don't know how many hours or weeks it was that I lay there counting hard. But the moonlight crept up that white arm, and it showed me a lead face and a terrible wound over the heart.

I could scarcely say that I was terror-stricken or anything like that. But somehow his eyes interested me so that I went right out of the window. I didn't need the sash. But it seemed easier to take it than leave it behind.

Now, let that teach you a lesson—I don't know just what it is. But at seventy years old I find that memory of peculiar value to me. I have been unconsciously guided by it all these years. Things that seemed pigeon-holed and remote are a perpetual influence. Yes, you're taught in so many ways. And you're so felicitously taught when you don't know it.

Here's something else that taught me a good deal.

When I was seventeen I was very bashful, and a sixteen-year-old girl came to stay a week with us. She was a peach, and I was seized with a happiness not of this world.

One evening my mother suggested that, to entertain her, I take her to the theatre. I didn't really like to, because I was seventeen and sensitive about appearing in the streets with a girl. I couldn't see my way to enjoying my delight in public. But we went.

I didn't feel very happy. I couldn't seem to keep my mind on the play. I became conscious, after a while, that that was due less to my lovely company than my boots. They were sweet to look upon, as smooth as skin, but fitted ten time as close. I got oblivious to the play and the girl and the other people and everything but my boots until—I hitched one partly off. The sensation was sensuously perfect: I couldn't help it. I had to get the other off, partly. Then I was obliged to get them off altogether, except that I kept my feet in the legs so they couldn't get away.

From that time I enjoyed the play. But the first thing I knew the curtain came down, like that, without my notice, and—I hadn't any boots on. What's more, they wouldn't go on. I tugged strenuously. And the people in our row got up and fussed and said things until the peach and I simply had to move on.

We moved—the girl on one arm and the boots under the other.

We walked home that way, sixteen blocks, with a retinue a mile long: Every time we passed a lamp-post, death gripped me at the throat. But we got home—and I had on white socks.

If I live to be nine hundred and ninety-nine years old I don't suppose I could ever forget that walk. I remember, it about as keenly as the chagrin I suffered on another occasion.

At one time in our domestic history we had a colored butler who had a failing. He could never remember to ask people who came to the door to state their business. So I used to suffer a good many calls unnecessarily.

One morning when I was especially busy he brought me a card engraved with a name I did not know. So I said, "What does he wish to see me for?" and Sylvester said, "Ah couldn't ask him, sah; he, wuz a genlinun." "Return instantly," I thundered, "and inquire his mission. Ask him what's his game." Well, Sylvester returned with the announcement that he had lightning-rods to sell. "Indeed," said I, "things are coming to a fine pass when lightning-rod agents send up engraved cards." "He has pictures," added Sylvester. "Pictures, indeed! He maybe peddling etchings. Has he a Russia leather case?" But Sylvester was too frightened to remember. I said; "I am going down to make it hot for that upstart!"

I went down the stairs, working up my temper all the way. When I got to the parlor I was in a fine frenzy concealed beneath a veneer of frigid courtesy. And when I looked in the door, sure enough he had a Russia leather case in his hand. But I didn't happen to notice that it was our Russia leather case.

And if you'd believe me, that man was sitting with a whole gallery of etchings spread out before him. But I didn't happen to notice that they were our etchings, spread out by some member of my family for some unguessed purpose.

Very curtly I asked the gentleman his business. With a surprised, timid manner he faltered that he had met my wife and daughter at Onteora, and they had asked him to call. Fine lie, I thought, and I froze him.

He seemed to be kind of non-plussed, and sat there fingering the etchings in the case until I told him he needn't bother, because we had those. That pleased him so much that he leaned over, in an embarrassed way, to pick up another from the floor. But I stopped him. I said, "We've got that, too." He seemed pitifully amazed, but I was congratulating myself on my great success.

Finally the gentleman asked where Mr. Winton lived; he'd met him in the mountains, too. So I said I'd show him gladly. And I did on the spot. And when he was gone I felt queer, because there were all his etchings spread out on the floor.

Well, my wife came in and asked me who had been in. I showed her the card, and told her all exultantly. To my dismay she nearly fainted. She told me he had been a most kind friend to them in the country, and had forgotten to tell me that he was expected our way. And she pushed me out of the door, and commanded me to get over to the Wintons in a hurry and get him back.

I came into the drawing-room, where Mrs. Winton was sitting up very stiff in a chair, beating me at my own game. Well, I began to put another light on things. Before many seconds Mrs. Winton saw it was time to change her temperature. In five minutes I had asked the man to luncheon, and she to dinner, and so on.

We made that fellow change his trip and stay a week, and we gave him the time of his life. Why, I don't believe we let him get sober the whole time.

I trust that you will carry away some good thought from these lessons I have given you, and that the memory of them will inspire you to higher things, and elevate you to plans far above the old—and—and—

And I tell you one thing, young ladies: I've had a better time with you to-day than with that peach fifty-three years ago.

TO THE PERSON
SITTING IN DARKNESS

"Christmas will dawn in the United States over a people full of hope and aspiration and good cheer. Such a condition means contentment and happiness. The carping grumbler who may here and there go forth will find few to listen to him. The majority will wonder what is the matter with him and pass on."—*New York Tribune*, on Christmas Eve.

From *The Sun*, of New York:

"The purpose of this article is not to describe the terrible offences against humanity committed in the name of Politics in some of the most notorious East Side districts. *They could not be described, even verbally.* But it is the intention to let the great mass of more or less careless citizens of this beautiful metropolis of the New World get some conception of the havoc and ruin wrought to man, woman and child in the most densely populated and least known section of the city. Name, date and place can be supplied to those of little faith—or to any man who feels himself aggrieved. It is a plain statement of record and observation, written without license and without garnish.

"Imagine, if you can, a section of the city territory completely dominated by one man, without whose permission neither legitimate nor illegitimate business can be conducted; *where illegitimate business is encouraged and legitimate business discouraged;* where the respectable residents have to fasten their doors and windows summer nights and sit in their rooms with asphyxiating air and 100-degree temperature, rather than try to catch the faint whiff of breeze in their natural breathing places, the stoops of their homes; *where naked women dance by night in the streets, and unsexed men prowl like vultures through the darkness on "business"* not only permitted but encouraged by the police; *where the education of infants begins with the knowledge of prostitution* and the training of little girls is training in the arts of Phryne; where *American* girls brought up with the refinements of *American* homes are imported from small towns up-State, Massachusetts, Connecticut and New Jersey, and kept as virtually prisoners as if they were locked up behind jail bars until they have lost all semblance of womanhood; *where small boys are taught to solicit for the women of disorderly houses;* where there is an organized society of young men *whose sole business in life is to corrupt young girls and turn them over to bawdy houses;* where men walking with their wives along the street are openly insulted; *where children that have adult diseases are the chief patrons of the hospitals and dispensaries;* where it is the rule, rather than the exception, that *murder, rape, robbery and theft go unpunished*—in short where the Premium of the most awful forms of Vice is the Profit of the politicians."

The following news from China appeared in *The Sun,* of New York, on Christmas Eve. The italics are mine:

"The Rev. Mr. Ament, of the American Board of Foreign Missions, has returned from a trip which he made for the purpose of collecting indemnities for damages done by Boxers. *Everywhere he went he compelled the Chinese to pay.* He says that all his native Christians are now provided for. He had 700 of them under his charge, and 300 were killed. He has *collected 300 taels for each* of these murders, and has *compelled full payment for all the property belonging to Christians* that was destroyed. He also assessed *fines* amounting to THIRTEEN TIMES the amount of the indemnity. *This money will be used for the propagation of the Gospel.*

"Mr. Ament declares that the compensation he has collected is *moderate,* when compared with the amount secured by the Catholics, who demand, in addition to money, *head for head.* They collect 500 taels for each murder of a Catholic. In the Wenchiu country, 680 Catholics were killed, and for this the European Catholics here demand 750,000 strings of cash and 680 *heads.*

"In the course of a conversation, Mr. Ament referred to the attitude of the missionaries toward the Chinese. He said:

"'I deny emphatically that the missionaries are *vindictive,* that they *generally* looted, or that they have done anything *since* the siege that *the circumstances did not demand.* I criticise the Americans. *The soft hand of the Americans is not as good as the mailed fist of the Germans.* If you deal with the Chinese with a soft hand they will take advantage of it.'

"The statement that the French Government will return the loot taken by the French soldiers, is the source of the greatest amusement here. The French soldiers were more systematic looters than the Germans, and it is a fact that to-day *Catholic Christians,* carrying French flags and armed with modern guns, *are looting villages* in the Province of Chili."

By happy luck, we get all these glad tidings on Christmas Eve—just in time to enable us to celebrate the day with proper gaiety and enthusiasm. Our spirits soar, and we find we can even make jokes: Taels I win, Heads you lose.

Our Reverend Ament is the right man in the right place. What we want of our missionaries out there is, not that they shall merely represent in their acts and persons the grace and gentleness and charity and loving kindness of our religion, but that they shall also represent the American spirit. The oldest Americans are the Pawnees. Macallum's History says:

"When a white Boxer kills a Pawnee and destroys his property, the other Pawnees do not trouble to seek *him* out, they kill any white person that comes along; also, they make some white village pay deceased's heirs the full cash value of deceased, together with full cash value of the property destroyed; they also make the village pay, in addition, *thirteen times* the value of that property into a fund for the dissemination of the Pawnee religion, which they regard as the best of all religions for the softening and humanizing of the heart of man. It is their idea that it is only fair and right that the innocent should be made to suffer for the guilty, and that it is better that ninety and nine innocent should suffer than that one guilty person should escape."

Our Reverend Ament is justifiably jealous of those enterprising Catholics, who not only get big money for each lost convert, but get "head for head" besides. But he should soothe himself with the reflection that the entirety of their exactions are for their own pockets, whereas he, less selfishly, devotes only 300 taels per head to that service, and gives the whole vast thirteen repetitions of the property-indemnity to the service of propagating the Gospel. His magnanimity has won him the approval of his nation, and will get him a monument. Let him be content with these rewards. We all hold him dear for manfully defending his fellow missionaries from exaggerated charges which were beginning to distress us, but which his testimony has so considerably modified that we can now contemplate them without noticeable pain. For now we know that, even before the siege, the missionaries were not "generally" out looting, and that, "since the siege," they have acted quite handsomely, except when "circumstances" crowded them. I am arranging for the monument. Subscriptions for it can be sent to the American Board; designs for it can be sent to me. Designs must allegorically set forth the Thirteen Reduplications of the Indemnity, and the Object for which they were exacted; as Ornaments, the designs must exhibit 680 Heads, so disposed as to give a pleasing and pretty effect; for the Catholics have done nicely, and are entitled to notice in the monument. Mottoes may be suggested, if any shall be discovered that will satisfactorily cover the ground.

Mr. Ament's financial feat of squeezing a thirteen-fold indemnity out of the pauper peasants to square other people's offenses, thus condemning them and their women and innocent little children to inevitable starvation and lingering death, in order that the blood-money so acquired might be *"used for the propagation of the Gospel,"* does not flutter my serenity; although the act and the words, taken together, concrete a blasphemy so hideous and so colossal that, without doubt, its mate is not findable in the history of this or of any other age. Yet, if a layman had done that thing and justified it with those words, I should have shuddered, I know. Or, if I had done the thing and said the words myself—however, the thought is unthinkable, irreverent as some imperfectly informed people think me. Sometimes an ordained minister sets out to be blasphemous. When this happens, the layman is out of the running; he stands no chance.

We have Mr. Ament's impassioned assurance that the missionaries are not "vindictive." Let us hope and pray that they will never become so, but will remain in the almost morbidly fair and just and gentle temper which is affording so much satisfaction to their brother and champion to-day.

The following is from the *New York Tribune* of Christmas Eve. It comes from that journal's Tokio correspondent. It has a strange and impudent sound, but the Japanese are but partially civilized as yet. When they become wholly civilized they will not talk so:

"The missionary question, of course, occupies a foremost place in the discussion. It is now felt as essential that the Western Powers take cognizance of the sentiment here, that religious invasions of Oriental countries by powerful Western organizations are tantamount to filibustering expeditions, and should not only be discountenanced, but that stern measures should be adopted for their suppression. The feeling here is that the missionary organizations constitute a constant menace to peaceful international relations."

Shall we? That is, shall we go on conferring our Civilization upon the peoples that sit in darkness, or shall we give those poor things a rest? Shall we bang right ahead in our old-time, loud, pious way, and commit the new century to the game; or shall we sober up and sit down and think it over first? Would it not be prudent to get our Civilization-tools together, and see how much stock is left on hand in the way of Glass Beads and Theology, and Maxim Guns and Hymn Books, and Trade-Gin and Torches of Progress and Enlightenment (patent adjustable ones, good to fire villages with, upon occasion), and balance the books, and arrive at the profit and loss, so that we may intelligently decide whether to continue the business or sell out the property and start a new Civilization Scheme on the proceeds?

Extending the Blessings of Civilization to our Brother who Sits in Darkness has been a good trade and has paid well, on the whole; and there is money in it yet, if carefully worked— but not enough, in my judgement, to make any considerable risk advisable. The People that Sit in Darkness are getting to be too scarce—too scarce and too shy. And such darkness as is now left is really of but an indifferent quality, and not dark enough for the game. The most of those People that Sit in Darkness have been furnished with more light than was good for them or profitable for us. We have been injudicious.

The Blessings-of-Civilization Trust, wisely and cautiously administered, is a Daisy. There is more money in it, more territory, more sovereignty, and other kinds of emolument, than there is in any other game that is played. But Christendom has been playing it badly of late years, and must certainly suffer by it, in my opinion. She has been so eager to get every stake that appeared on the green cloth, that the People who Sit in Darkness have noticed it—they have noticed it, and have begun to show alarm. They have become suspicious of the Blessings of Civilization. More—they have begun to examine them. This is not well. The Blessings of Civilization are all right, and a good commercial property; there could not be a better, in a dim light. In the right kind of a light, and at a proper distance, with the goods a little out of focus, they furnish this desirable exhibit to the Gentlemen who Sit in Darkness:

LOVE,
LAW AND ORDER,

JUSTICE,
LIBERTY,
GENTLENESS,
EQUALITY,
CHRISTIANITY,
HONORABLE DEALING,
PROTECTION TO THE WEAK,
MERCY,
TEMPERANCE,
EDUCATION,

—and so on.

There. Is it good? Sir, it is pie. It will bring into camp any idiot that sits in darkness anywhere. But not if we adulterate it. It is proper to be emphatic upon that point. This brand is strictly for Export—apparently. *Apparently.* Privately and confidentially, it is nothing of the kind. Privately and confidentially, it is merely an outside cover, gay and pretty and attractive, displaying the special patterns of our Civilization which we reserve for Home Consumption, while *inside* the bale is the Actual Thing that the Customer Sitting in Darkness buys with his blood and tears and land and liberty. That Actual Thing is, indeed, Civilization, but it is only for Export. Is there a difference between the two brands? In some of the details, yes.

We all know that the Business is being ruined. The reason is not far to seek. It is because our Mr. McKinley, and Mr. Chamberlain, and the Kaiser, and the Czar and the French have been exporting the Actual Thing *with the outside cover left off.* This is bad for the Game. It shows that these new players of it are not sufficiently acquainted with it.

It is a distress to look on and note the mismoves, they are so strange and so awkward. Mr. Chamberlain manufactures a war out of materials so inadequate and so fanciful that they make the boxes grieve and the gallery laugh, and he tries hard to persuade himself that it isn't purely a private raid for cash, but has a sort of dim, vague respectability about it somewhere, if he could only find the spot; and that, by and by, he can scour the flag clean again after he has finished dragging it through the mud, and make it shine and flash in the vault of heaven once more as it had shone and flashed there a thousand years in the world's respect until he laid his unfaithful hand upon it. It is bad play—bad. For it exposes the Actual Thing to Them that Sit in Darkness, and they say: "What! Christian against Christian? And only for money? Is *this* a case of magnanimity, forbearance, love, gentleness, mercy, protection of the weak—this strange and over-showy onslaught of an elephant upon a nest of field-mice, on the pretext that the mice had squeaked an insolence at him—conduct which 'no self-respecting government could allow to pass unavenged?' as Mr. Chamberlain said. Was that a good pretext in a small case, when it had not been a good pretext in a large one?—for only recently Russia had affronted the elephant three times and survived alive and unsmitten. Is this Civilization and Progress? Is it something better than we already possess? These harryings and burnings and desert-makings in the Transvaal—is this an improvement on our darkness? Is it, perhaps, possible that there are two kinds of Civilization—one for home consumption and one for the heathen market?"

Then They that Sit in Darkness are troubled, and shake their heads; and they read this extract from a letter of a British private, recounting his exploits in one of Methuen's victories, some days before the affair of Magersfontein, and they are troubled again:

"We tore up the hill and into the intrenchments, and the Boers saw we had them; so they dropped their guns and went down on their knees and put up their hands clasped, and begged for mercy. And we gave it them—*with the long spoon.*"

The long spoon is the bayonet. See *Lloyd's Weekly,* London, of those days. The same number—and the same column—contained some quite unconscious satire in the form of shocked and bitter upbraidings of the Boers for their brutalities and inhumanities!

Next, to our heavy damage, the Kaiser went to playing the game without first mastering it. He lost a couple of missionaries in a riot in Shantung, and in his account he made an overcharge for them. China had to pay a hundred thousand dollars apiece for them, in money; twelve miles of territory, containing several millions of inhabitants and worth twenty million dollars; and to build a monument, and also a Christian church; whereas the people of China could have been depended upon to remember the missionaries without the help of these expensive memorials. This was all bad play. Bad, because it would not, and could not, and will not now or ever, deceive the Person Sitting in Darkness. He knows that it was an overcharge. He knows that a missionary is like any other man: he is worth merely what you can supply his place for, and no more. He is useful, but so is a doctor, so is a sheriff, so is an editor; but a just Emperor does not charge war-prices for such. A diligent, intelligent, but obscure missionary, and a diligent, intelligent country editor are worth much, and we know it; but they are not worth the earth. We esteem such an editor, and we are sorry to see him go; but, when he goes, we should consider twelve miles of territory, and a church, and a fortune, over-compensation for his loss. I mean, if he was a Chinese editor, and we had to settle for him. It is no proper figure for an editor or a missionary; one can get shop-worn kings for less. It was bad play on the Kaiser's part. It got this property, true; but it *produced the Chinese revolt,* the indignant uprising of China's traduced patriots, the Boxers. The results have been expensive to Germany, and to the other Disseminators of Progress and the Blessings of Civilization.

The Kaiser's claim was paid, yet it was bad play, for it could not fail to have an evil effect upon Persons Sitting in Darkness in China. They would muse upon the event, and be likely to say: "Civilization is gracious and beautiful, for such is its reputation; but can we afford it? There are rich Chinamen, perhaps they could afford it; but this tax is not laid upon them, it is laid upon the peasants of Shantung; it is they that must pay this mighty sum, and their wages are but four cents a day. Is this a better civilization than ours, and holier and higher and nobler? Is not this rapacity? Is not this extortion? Would Germany charge America two hundred thousand dollars for two missionaries, and shake the mailed fist in her face, and send warships, and send soldiers, and say: 'Seize twelve miles of territory, worth twenty millions of dollars, as additional pay for the missionaries; and make those peasants build a monument to the missionaries, and a costly Christian church to remember them by?' And later would Germany say to her soldiers: 'March through America and slay, *giving no quarter;* make the German face there, as has been our Hun-face here, a terror for a thousand years; march through the Great Republic and slay, slay, slay, carving a road for our offended religion through its heart and bowels?' Would Germany do like this to America, to England, to France, to Russia? Or only to China the helpless— imitating the elephant's assault upon the field-mice? Had we better invest in this Civilization—this Civilization which called Napoleon a buccaneer for carrying off Venice's bronze horses, but which steals our ancient astronomical instruments from our walls, and goes looting like common bandits—that is, all the alien soldiers except America's; and (Americans again excepted) storms frightened villages and cables the result to glad journals at home every day: 'Chinese losses, 450 killed; ours, *one officer and two men wounded.* Shall proceed against neighboring village to-morrow, where a *massacre* is reported.' Can we afford Civilization?"

And, next, Russia must go and play the game injudiciously. She affronts England once or twice—with the Person Sitting in Darkness observing and noting; by moral assistance of France and Germany, she robs Japan of her hard-earned spoil, all swimming in Chinese blood—Port Arthur—with the Person again observing and noting; then she seizes Manchuria, raids its villages, and chokes its great river with the swollen corpses of countless massacred peasants—that astonished Person still observing and noting. And perhaps he is saying to himself: "It is yet *another* Civilized Power, with its banner of the Prince of Peace in one hand and its loot-basket and its butcher-knife in the other. Is there no salvation for us but to adopt Civilization and lift ourselves down to its level?"

And by and by comes America, and our Master of the Game plays it badly—plays it as Mr. Chamberlain was playing it in South Africa. It was a mistake to do that; also, it was one which was quite unlooked for in a Master who was playing it so well in Cuba. In Cuba, he was playing the usual and regular *American* game, and it was winning, for there is no way to beat it. The Master, contemplating Cuba, said: "Here is an oppressed and friendless little nation which is willing to fight to be free; we go partners, and put up the strength of seventy million sympathizers and the resources of the United States: play!" Nothing but Europe combined could call that hand: and Europe cannot combine on anything. There, in Cuba, he was following our great traditions in a way which made us very proud of him, and proud of the deep dissatisfaction which his play was provoking in Continental Europe. Moved by a high inspiration, he threw out those stirring words which proclaimed that forcible annexation would be "criminal aggression;" and in that utterance fired another "shot heard round the world." The memory of that fine saying will be outlived by the remembrance of no act of his but one—that he forgot it within the twelvemonth, and its honorable gospel along with it.

For, presently, came the Philippine temptation. It was strong; it was too strong, and he made that bad mistake: he played the European game, the Chamberlain game. It was a pity; it was a great pity, that error; that one grievous error, that irrevocable error. For it was the very place and time to play the American game again. And at no cost. Rich winnings to be gathered in, too; rich and permanent; indestructible; a fortune transmissible forever to the children of the flag. Not land, not money, not dominion—no, something worth many times more than that dross: our share, the spectacle of a nation of long harassed and persecuted slaves set free through our influence; our posterity's share, the golden memory of that fair deed. The game was in our hands. If it had been played according to the American rules, Dewey would have sailed away from Manila as soon as he had destroyed the Spanish fleet—after putting up a sign on shore guaranteeing foreign property and life against damage by the Filipinos, and warning the Powers that interference with the emancipated patriots would be regarded as an act unfriendly to the United States. The Powers cannot combine, in even a bad cause, and the sign would not have been molested.

Dewey could have gone about his affairs elsewhere, and left the competent Filipino army to starve out the little Spanish garrison and send it home, and the Filipino citizens to set up the form of government they might prefer, and deal with the friars and their doubtful acquisitions according to Filipino ideas of fairness and justice—ideas which have since been tested and found to be of as high an order as any that prevail in Europe or America.

But we played the Chamberlain game, and lost the chance to add another Cuba and another honorable deed to our good record.

The more we examine the mistake, the more clearly we perceive that it is going to be bad for the Business. The Person Sitting in Darkness is almost sure to say: "There is something curious about this—curious and unaccountable. There must be two Americas: one that sets the captive free, and one that takes a once-captive's new freedom away from him, and picks a quarrel with him with nothing to found it on; then kills him to get his land."

The truth is, the Person Sitting in Darkness *is* saying things like that; and for the sake of the Business we must persuade him to look at the Philippine matter in another and healthier way. We must arrange his opinions for him. I believe it can be done; for Mr. Chamberlain has arranged England's opinion of the South African matter, and done it most cleverly and successfully. He presented the facts—some of the facts—and showed those confiding people what the facts meant. He did it statistically, which is a good way. He used the formula: "Twice 2 are 14, and 2 from 9 leaves 35." Figures are effective; figures will convince the elect.

Now, my plan is a still bolder one than Mr. Chamberlain's, though apparently a copy of it. Let us be franker than Mr. Chamberlain; let us audaciously present the whole of the facts, shirking none, then explain them according to Mr. Chamberlain's formula. This daring truthfulness will astonish and dazzle the Person Sitting in Darkness, and he will take the Explanation down before his mental vision has had time to get back into focus. Let us say to him:

"Our case is simple. On the 1st of May, Dewey destroyed the Spanish fleet. This left the Archipelago in the hands of its proper and rightful owners, the Filipino nation. Their army numbered 30,000 men, and they were competent to whip out or starve out the little Spanish garrison; then the people could set up a government of their own devising. Our traditions required that Dewey should now set up his warning sign, and go away. But the Master of the Game happened to think of another plan— the European plan. He acted upon it. This was, to send out an army—ostensibly to help the native patriots put the finishing touch upon their long and plucky struggle for independence, but really to take their land away from them and keep it. That is, in the interest of Progress and Civilization. The plan developed, stage by stage, and quite satisfactorily. We entered into a military alliance with the trusting Filipinos, and they hemmed in Manila on the land side, and by their valuable help the place, with its garrison of 8,000 or 10,000 Spaniards, was captured—a thing which we could not have accomplished unaided at that time. We got their help by—by ingenuity. We knew they were fighting for their independence, and that they had been at it for two years. We knew they supposed that we also were fighting in their worthy cause—just as we had helped the Cubans fight for

Cuban independence—and we allowed them to go on thinking so. *Until Manila was ours and we could get along without them.* Then we showed our hand. Of course, they were surprised—that was natural; surprised and disappointed; disappointed and grieved. To them it looked un-American; uncharacteristic; foreign to our established traditions. And this was natural, too; for we were only playing the American Game in public—in private it was the European. It was neatly done, very neatly, and it bewildered them. They could not understand it; for we had been so friendly—so affectionate, even—with those simple-minded patriots! We, our own selves, had brought back out of exile their leader, their hero, their hope, their Washington—Aguinaldo; brought him in a warship, in high honor, under the sacred shelter and hospitality of the flag; brought him back and restored him to his people, and got their moving and eloquent gratitude for it. Yes, we had been so friendly to them, and had heartened them up in so many ways! We had lent them guns and ammunition; advised with them; exchanged pleasant courtesies with them; placed our sick and wounded in their kindly care; entrusted our Spanish prisoners to their humane and honest hands; fought shoulder to shoulder with them against "the common enemy" (our own phrase); praised their courage, praised their gallantry, praised their mercifulness, praised their fine and honorable conduct; borrowed their trenches, borrowed strong positions which they had previously captured from the Spaniard; petted them, lied to them—officially proclaiming that our land and naval forces came to give them their freedom and displace the bad Spanish Government—fooled them, used them until we needed them no longer; then derided the sucked orange and threw it away. We kept the positions which we had beguiled them of; by and by, we moved a force forward and overlapped patriot ground—a clever thought, for we needed trouble, and this would produce it. A Filipino soldier, crossing the ground, where no one had a right to forbid him, was shot by our sentry. The badgered patriots resented this with arms, without waiting

to know whether Aguinaldo, who was absent, would approve
or not. Aguinaldo did not approve; but that availed nothing.
What we wanted, in the interest of Progress and Civilization,
was the Archipelago, unencumbered by patriots struggling for
independence; and War was what we needed. We clinched our
opportunity. It is Mr. Chamberlain's case over again—at least in
its motive and intention; and we played the game as adroitly as
he played it himself."

At this point in our frank statement of fact to the Person
Sitting in Darkness, we should throw in a little trade-taffy
about the Blessings of Civilization—for a change, and for the
refreshment of his spirit—then go on with our tale:

"We and the patriots having captured Manila, Spain's
ownership of the Archipelago and her sovereignty over it were at
an end—obliterated—annihilated—not a rag or shred of either
remaining behind. It was then that we conceived the divinely
humorous idea of *buying* both of these spectres from Spain! [It is
quite safe to confess this to the Person Sitting in Darkness, since
neither he nor any other sane person will believe it.] In buying
those ghosts for twenty millions, we also contracted to take care
of the friars and their accumulations. I think we also agreed to
propagate leprosy and smallpox, but as to this there is doubt. But
it is not important; persons afflicted with the friars do not mind
other diseases.

"With our Treaty ratified, Manila subdued, and our Ghosts
secured, we had no further use for Aguinaldo and the owners
of the Archipelago. We forced a war, and we have been hunting
America's guest and ally through the woods and swamps
ever since."

At this point in the tale, it will be well to boast a little of
our war-work and our heroisms in the field, so as to make our
performance look as fine as England's in South Africa; but I
believe it will not be best to emphasize this too much. We must
be cautious. Of course, we must read the war-telegrams to the
Person, in order to keep up our frankness; but we can throw an

air of humorousness over them, and that will modify their grim eloquence a little, and their rather indiscreet exhibitions of gory exultation. Before reading to him the following display heads of the dispatches of November 18, 1900, it will be well to practice on them in private first, so as to get the right tang of lightness and gaiety into them:

"ADMINISTRATION WEARY OF PROTRACTED HOSTILITIES!"

"REAL WAR AHEAD FOR FILIPINO REBELS!"[5]

"WILL SHOW NO MERCY!"

"KITCHENER'S PLAN ADOPTED!"

Kitchener knows how to handle disagreeable people who are fighting for their homes and their liberties, and we must let on that we are merely imitating Kitchener, and have no national interest in the matter, further than to get ourselves admired by the Great Family of Nations, in which august company our Master of the Game has bought a place for us in the back row.

Of course, we must not venture to ignore our General MacArthur's reports—oh, why do they keep on printing those embarrassing things?—we must drop them trippingly from the tongue and take the chances:

"During the last ten months our losses have been 268 killed and 750 wounded; Filipino loss, *three thousand two hundred and twenty-seven killed,* and 694 wounded."

We must stand ready to grab the Person Sitting in Darkness, for he will swoon away at this confession, saying: "Good God, those 'niggers' spare their wounded, and the Americans

5   Rebels!" Mumble that funny word—Don't let the Person catch it distinctly."

110

massacre theirs!"

We must bring him to, and coax him and coddle him, and assure him that the ways of Providence are best, and that it would not become us to find fault with them; and then, to show him that we are only imitators, not originators, we must read the following passage from the letter of an American soldier-lad in the Philippines to his mother, published in *Public Opinion*, of Decorah, Iowa, describing the finish of a victorious battle:

> "WE NEVER LEFT ONE ALIVE. IF ONE WAS
> WOUNDED, WE WOULD RUN OUR BAYONETS
> THROUGH HIM."

Having now laid all the historical facts before the Person Sitting in Darkness, we should bring him to again, and explain them to him. We should say to him:

"They look doubtful, but in reality they are not. There have been lies; yes, but they were told in a good cause. We have been treacherous; but that was only in order that real good might come out of apparent evil. True, we have crushed a deceived and confiding people; we have turned against the weak and the friendless who trusted us; we have stamped out a just and intelligent and well-ordered republic; we have stabbed an ally in the back and slapped the face of a guest; we have bought a Shadow from an enemy that hadn't it to sell; we have robbed a trusting friend of his land and his liberty; we have invited our clean young men to shoulder a discredited musket and do bandit's work under a flag which bandits have been accustomed to fear, not to follow; we have debauched America's honor and blackened her face before the world; but each detail was for the best. We know this. The Head of every State and Sovereignty in Christendom and ninety per cent. of every legislative body in Christendom, including our Congress and our fifty State Legislatures, are members not only of the church, but also of the Blessings-of-Civilization Trust. This world-girdling accumulation of trained morals, high principles, and justice, cannot do an unright thing, an unfair thing, an ungenerous thing, an unclean thing. It knows what it is about. Give yourself no uneasiness; it is all right."

Now then, that will convince the Person. You will see. It will restore the Business. Also, it will elect the Master of the Game to the vacant place in the Trinity of our national gods; and there on their high thrones the Three will sit, age after age, in the people's sight, each bearing the Emblem of his service: Washington, the Sword of the Liberator; Lincoln, the Slave's Broken Chains; the Master, the Chains Repaired.

It will give the Business a splendid new start. You will see.

Everything is prosperous, now; everything is just as we should wish it. We have got the Archipelago, and we shall never give it up. Also, we have every reason to hope that we shall have an opportunity before very long to slip out of our Congressional contract with Cuba and give her something better in the place of it. It is a rich country, and many of us are already beginning to see that the contract was a sentimental mistake. But now— right now—is the best time to do some profitable rehabilitating work—work that will set us up and make us comfortable, and discourage gossip. We cannot conceal from ourselves that, privately, we are a little troubled about our uniform. It is one of our prides; it is acquainted with honor; it is familiar with great deeds and noble; we love it, we revere it; and so this errand it is on makes us uneasy. And our flag—another pride of ours, our chiefest! We have worshipped it so; and when we have seen it in far lands—glimpsing it unexpectedly in that strange sky, waving its welcome and benediction to us—we have caught our breath, and uncovered our heads, and couldn't speak, for a moment, for the thought of what it was to us and the great ideals it stood for. Indeed, we *must* do something about these things; we must not have the flag out there, and the uniform. They are not needed there; we can manage in some other way. England manages, as regards the uniform, and so can we. We have to send soldiers—

we can't get out of that—but we can disguise them. It is the way England does in South Africa. Even Mr. Chamberlain himself takes pride in England's honorable uniform, and makes the army down there wear an ugly and odious and appropriate disguise, of yellow stuff such as quarantine flags are made of, and which are hoisted to warn the healthy away from unclean disease and repulsive death. This cloth is called khaki. We could adopt it. It is light, comfortable, grotesque, and deceives the enemy, for he cannot conceive of a soldier being concealed in it.

And as for a flag for the Philippine Province, it is easily managed. We can have a special one—our States do it: we can have just our usual flag, with the white stripes painted black and the stars replaced by the skull and cross-bones.

And we do not need that Civil Commission out there. Having no powers, it has to invent them, and that kind of work cannot be effectively done by just anybody; an expert is required. Mr. Croker can be spared. We do not want the United States represented there, but only the Game.

By help of these suggested amendments, Progress and Civilization in that country can have a boom, and it will take in the Persons who are Sitting in Darkness, and we can resume Business at the old stand.

MARK TWAIN.

First published in 1901

Printed in Great Britain
by Amazon

21239495R00068